BUDDHA MOM

JEREMY P. TARCHER/PENGUIN
a member of
Penguin Group (USA) Inc.
New York

BUDDHA MOM

A Journey Through
Mindful Mothering

JACQUELINE KRAMER

Most Tarcher/Penguin books are available at special
quantity discounts for bulk purchase for sales promo-
tions, premiums, fund-raising, and educational needs.
Special books or book excerpts also can be created to fit
specific needs. For details, write: Penguin Group (USA) Inc.
Special Markets, 375 Hudson Street, New York, NY
10014.

Jeremy P. Tarcher/Penguin
a member of
Penguin Group (USA) Inc.
375 Hudson Street
New York, NY 10014
www.penguin.com

First trade paperback edition 2004

The Library of Congress catalogued the hardcover edition as follows:
Kramer, Jacqueline.
Buddha Mom : a journey through mindful mothering /
Jacqueline Kramer.
p. cm.
ISBN 1-58542-217-7
1. Mothers—Religious life. 2. Religious life—
Buddhism. 3. Motherhood—Religious aspects—
Buddhism. I. Title.

BQ5440.K73   2003   2002034771
294.3'4441—dc21

ISBN 1-58542-294-0 (Paperback edition)

Printed in the United States of America
1   3   5   7   9   10   8   6   4   2

BOOK DESIGN BY AMANDA DEWEY

ACKNOWLEDGMENTS

I am grateful for everyone and everything in my life that has brought me to this point.

I am grateful to Anagarika Dhammadina, Sister Ayya Khema, Thich Nhat Hanh, Bikku Mangala, the Venerable Ananda Maitreya, Bante Punnaji, and all the other monks and nuns who shared the precious jewel of the Buddha's teachings;

I am grateful to all the Religious Science Practitioners who wrap me in their love;

I am grateful to Louis Armstrong for helping me feel happy when all else fails;

I am grateful to my mother for modeling impeccability, the love of learning, and the importance of being a mench;

I am grateful to my father who, with the heart of a poet, taught me about power and supported me through thick and thin;

I am grateful to my brother Jono for showing me how delicious words can be;

I am grateful to my brother Greg for being my best friend in this world or any other, and for being a well at which I drink the Buddha's teachings;

I am grateful to all those who helped me hone this manuscript in its early stages, particularly Bante Selawhimila, Jack Kornfield, and Allysa Lukara;

I am grateful to chronic fatigue syndrome for keeping my seat to the writing bench so that this book could become a reality;

I am grateful to Hal Zina Bennett for being an honest, gentle guide through the editing process;

I am grateful to Joel Fotinos for midwifing this book with love and brilliance;

I am grateful to my darling Nicole for letting me share this intimate portrait of our relationship and for being so sweet and wise;

I am grateful to the garden, trees, wind, rocks, birds, bushes, sun, flowers, stars, bugs, and the moon for reminding me that life is good;

I am grateful to all mothers everywhere who are too busy living this book to write it.

If this book helps one mother in one moment it will have been worth all the effort it took to write it. Thank you for sharing this journey with me!

This book is dedicated to my first spiritual teacher and mother, Rose, and to all mothers everywhere. Bless you for all you do. I devote the merit of this work to the well-being of all sentient beings.

CONTENTS

PREFACE ✖

by Nicole Serena Silver

The author of this book is not only my best friend; she is my mother too. I view our relationship as unique. I have always felt like we are equals. We both give and receive in the same proportions. I have always felt I could talk to her about anything. I am just now seeing, at the age of twenty-one, my friends getting to a point of being comfortable with their parents and starting a friendship. I know that the relationship my mother and I have has also inspired some of my friends and ex-boyfriends to begin this process of maturity and unity among their parents. Unfortunately, not all parents are receptive to this kind of relationship, and lacking the closeness and trust that my mother and I have enjoyed, this can cause damage that sometimes is never healed. When I reflect on this, it shows me that I am truly blessed. I guess I could say that I have also experienced a more distant and less caring relationship with my father. He never took the step to open up to the development of our relationship.

One thing that needs to be acknowledged is the amount of love that my mother possesses. We come from generations of motherly women. I am now seeing it blossom within myself. I was born an only child but did not lead an only-child life. My mother treated all my friends as if they were her own children. In our house, there was a sense of love and comfort for everyone who ever walked in the door. My best friend would always come over when she was sick because she knew my mom would nurture her, and this was the feeling my friends always associated with my mom. They knew they could always come to her, no matter what. My mother and I were also foster parents for a portion of my life. The experience of seeing what these children in the foster-care system go through made me appreciate my life to the fullest extent, and I got the chance to feel what it would be like to have a younger brother or sister.

In my younger days I took my mom for granted. I was very angry and rebellious throughout junior high due to my anger and disappointment with my father's and my relationship. I was always getting in trouble and disrespecting my mother. I remember the many times that I would call her nasty names or tell her I hated her. To this day, I still feel bad about those years. I'm surprised she didn't lose all her hair in the process! I know she felt lost trying to help me. The truth is only I could help myself. She guided me in the right direction to overcome my wounds. What helped me the most was a wilderness survival program my mother enrolled me in. It had to be the best experience for me. I dug deep into the core of my problems and came to realizations about my past actions and how I was going to redirect my present actions.

My mother has taught me how to maintain physical, mental, and spiritual health. She has taught me by example. She eats healthily, does yoga, keeps a positive attitude, and meditates every morning. I was never forced to accept her way of life or practice it against my will. She provided me the freedom to simply observe or join in. Now, as an adult, I admire these qualities and find myself reaching for the levels of development that my mom has achieved. This is a recent development in my goals. As a teenager, I felt the need to separate myself from her in order to develop my own values and place in life. Today, I am tremendously grateful for all that she has provided. She has taught me so many wonderful values that I apply in my life.

I read this book alongside my mother as she was working on the final rewrites. It was a time for me to sit back and look at all that she has done for me. It just made my vision of her even more vibrant with love and respect. She is one of the purest and most giving human beings I have ever known. My friends, who knew her when I was growing up, will also vouch for that. I know if I ever run into any problems that I need help solving, the first person I would turn to is my mother. She is never one to take sides. With her, I get an honest answer that I sometimes don't want to hear, but which ultimately helps me find my own best solution.

It is comforting to know that someone will always be there for you no matter what. I could not be more content in this life she has provided me with. To all you new mothers out there I hope this book helps you and your child form a wonderful relationship.

Maybe, too, it will help you remember that it is not always going to be easy. I am confident in saying that the advice given in this book will help you through all the major challenges of motherhood.

And to my mom, there are not enough words to express my love and thanks for all you have given me. You have given me the gift of life with all the nourishment I have ever needed. I love you.

SETTING FOOT
on the PATH

PREGNANCY ﹍

Turning Inward

Pregnancy is regarded as a spiritual practice in the Orient. Traditionally it takes precedence over other Tao's or practices and is preeminent for at least nine months. . . . It is felt that the mother should spend her time, as much as possible, in prayer and contemplation. That she should surround herself with pleasant things: physically, emotionally and mentally. . . . She should practice as much meritorious activity as possible such as charity, morality, patience, etc. She should also seek the blessings of the holy places and objects. This is because of the connection from the mother's mind to the infant's through the Chong-mo or penetrating channel.

BOB FLAWS, *The Path of Pregnancy*
(Boulder, Colorado: Blue Poppy Press, 1982)

Drifting off to sleep, leaving the noises of the world behind me, I began to enter dreamtime reality. I dreamt that I was walking in a field full of sharp purple thistle, yellow mustard weed, and tall thick grasses. My mother was walking in front of me. Everything around was bright and colorful. The grass was kelly green and the sky was cobalt blue with a few wisps of clouds moving lazily through it. I looked down at my pregnant belly and felt determined to make it safely to the other side of the field. I vowed to my baby that "I will be your bed until you awaken." We came to the end of the field, and my mother placed around my head a wreath of roses with thorns attached. I walked on, alone in the blossoming field. When I awoke I felt something strange stirring in my body.

A couple of days after the dream, on a hot, sticky August afternoon, my body felt tender and strangely sensitive. I felt like Alice in Wonderland who had just eaten cake and was suddenly growing all out of proportion. Nausea overwhelmed me as rapid electrifying changes churned in my body and my psyche. I knew I was pregnant. I felt excited. I couldn't believe that this miracle was really happening inside my previously stable body. I was fearful. Something that I had no control over had begun, and it was overtaking me. I was helpless to stop it or even to slow it down. I felt inadequate. How could I be a mother, I who had only been a daughter? What an awesome responsibility! Would I be capable of fulfilling it? Everything seemed to be twisting, turning, and changing. My senses were keenly enhanced. Some quiet nights I would lie awake in bed, aware of my baby's presence, amazed by how little I had to do with this process and overwhelmed by the power of Nature fulfilling itself through me. I felt terrified by the irreversibility of this tremendous force within me.

This feeling of being moved by an invisible power was familiar to me. Every year for the past twenty years I have gone on ten-day Vipassana meditation retreats with my teacher, Anagarika Dhamma Dinna. All I knew about Buddhism when I went on my first retreat was what I had read in a book of Zen stories I carried around in my purse when I was sixteen. But it had been my brother Greg, when I was twenty-five years old, who'd inspired me to go on retreat. He had just returned from his first retreat, and I saw him change before my eyes, becoming softer and brighter. When I asked him what was creating this perceptible shift in him he told me about his new teacher, Anagarika, and the retreat he had gone on. I knew immediately that this was something I needed to do. For as long as I could remember I had felt so much anger within me, just a general, lingering anger, and I didn't understand it. I knew this anger was an ever-present undercurrent. I wanted to let go of it but didn't know how. After talking with my brother I had a feeling that these retreats might help me.

I went to my first retreat blindly, naively, and thank God for that! Had I known what I was in for I might not have made the trip up north to that chilly isolated retreat center. Just as with retreat, had I known what I was in for with pregnancy and birthing I wonder if I would have chosen to go through that fire. Like the fool card in the tarot deck, taking a step off the precipice I find myself carelessly leaping into my greatest growth experiences with blissful ignorance. At the retreat center I was greeted at the gate by Anagarika herself. Within five minutes of meeting her she confronted me with "So, you're in the hate group." She complained about having to be a *lion tamer* on top of everything else. She clearly did not like me, so I thought, and so I still wonder to this day. But, no matter, she said exactly what I needed to hear in order to get right down to the business of clearing up my murky consciousness.

During that retreat there were many times I just wanted to scream, to leave. I often felt overwhelmed by the emotional forces arising within me. Yet I continued, year after year, turning inward for healing and insight. Over time I watched as painful dark areas of my psyche arose and dissolved and the precious jewel of my being peeked out. From the experience of turning inward during meditation retreats, with no one to blame for what I was feeling, I learned to take responsibility for my thoughts and feelings. I learned to see everything that crossed my path, painful and pleasurable, as an opportunity for spiritual growth.

When I am at the beginning of a profound change, like a retreat or like pregnancy, my attention turns away from everyday external realities and focuses instead on my inner core. These are times of clearing and bright seeing. Whether the inward turning comes about by choice, as in going on a retreat, or whether it is thrust upon me, as in pregnancy, the process is the same. A window of opportunity is opened. Life is always moving, sometimes in still, gentle rhythms and sometimes powerfully like a tsunami. I have no control over the fact that life is always changing and rearranging everything around and within me. I do, however, have control over how I ride the waves.

On retreat I learned about the five hindrances to meditation. The Buddha described these as: (1) anger or ill will, (2) sloth or laziness, (3) lust or sensual desire, (4) doubt, and (5) restlessness. They are called hindrances because they impede the arising of calm in the mind. I learned to watch for hinderances on retreat and watched in surprise as they arose with equal force during pregnancy. Old feelings of anger and restlessness and doubt began to assert themselves. Sensual desire became a mental state that tied me to the earth, not desirable for a monk or nun but important for a mother. Sloth was eradicated by the activity of life moving through me and demanding my presence. Just as with the dream that signaled my pregnancy, my dreams during pregnancy became vivid and intense as old emotions rose to the surface to be healed.

Being pregnant was a roller-coaster ride as my body and psyche carried me through a seemingly endless series of changes. As any mother knows, pregnancy is one of the most life-altering experiences a woman ever goes through. Isadora Duncan wrote: "I sometimes felt an excess of strength and prowess, but on other days, when the sky was grey and the cold North sea waves were angry, I had sudden, sinking moods when I felt myself some poor animal in a mighty trap and I struggled with an overwhelming desire to escape, escape. Where?"

As my body turned me inward I became increasingly sensitive to the effects of anger and discord. Unkindness or negativity, which bothered me only slightly before, had now become unbearable. I was painfully aware of how counterproductive unkindness is. Little nasty jokes followed by "I'm only joking" became barbs; criticism tore at my heart. Sometimes pregnant women are accused of being hypersensitive. Maybe they are just more in touch with a deeper level of emotional reality.

Before becoming pregnant I had carefully considered the two paths a spiritual aspirant can take: the monastic path and the path of the householder. On the monastic path the spiritual aspirant tries to minimize distractions in order to focus on meditation and enlightenment. But I had chosen the path of the householder. Here my challenge was to use these "distractions" as fuel for the spiritual fire within me. Sensuality was one of these potent fuels. Pregnancy is a sensual, sexual state of being. Instead of rejecting the distraction of lust, I was encouraged to consciously embrace my sensuality. I was encouraged to explore my divinity through my elemental earthy nature. What the Buddha called the hindrance of lust, or the distraction of sensuality, became, during my pregnancy, a pathway into my feminine divinity.

By the fourth month of my pregnancy, my body had adjusted to the constant changes and had become warm and receptive. I felt luminous, like an orchid in bloom. It was strange to see my nymphlike body becoming round and ripe and fruitful. My breasts filled with maternal milk and my flat, hard belly became soft and abundant. My body felt deliciously sensual as it rippled with new sensations.

Lying on my side in a patch of afternoon sun, I was awakened by tiny kicks inside my abdomen. My body stretched to make room for its ripening fruit. I heard the music of wind chimes wafting in the breeze. The first thing I saw was the exaggerated clarity of a patch of wooden floor with a spotlight of sun on it. The sun pouring down on my body emphasized the aliveness of my skin. I felt the baby restlessly stretching. How sweet and strange those kicks were from this creature my body was hosting! While lying in a patch of bright warm sun, hearing the sound of the wind chimes, sinking into the comfort of my couch, I felt deeply contented. I was living in the present with no yearnings or desires for anything but the simple moment, just as when I settle into meditation on retreat. I became alert and relaxed like a cat lounging on the deck with no ambition, just drinking in the electricity of each moment.

Plans, schedules, goals, all seemed meaningless to me. At those precious moments I felt deep satisfaction living in the feminine realm of timelessness. Feminine time is the ever-present now. Like so many others in our culture I was raised to focus on *doing,* but now I was being invited to cultivate the *art of being.* The sensuality of pregnancy helped me turn inward, helping me to connect more deeply with the present moment, which is also the goal of meditation practice.

I loved being pregnant. I loved the power and sensuality of it. I loved taking a step out of my egocentric world into a realm where I was just a function of Nature, one piece of an enormous puzzle. While pregnant I was in love with the magic, the physicality, the doubt and rapture of life. Sensations of life and love swept me away, and I didn't know where or when I would land. Pregnancy brought me into the moment and back to my elemental, sensual earthiness, connecting me with the wisdom and perfection of Nature.

I found myself swinging back and forth between this primal, visceral self who loved the pregnancy and an intellectual, civilized, ego-centered self who feared it. I shifted between relaxing into the sensual, flowing changes of my body and contracting with fear because of my desire to be in control. The fear of losing control was fertile ground for the hindrance of doubt, which became my biggest emotional challenge during pregnancy. At times I thought of all these changes as an earthquake, and as it slowly rumbled through my body, I knew the vibrations would get stronger and stronger. But I didn't know how powerful this force would finally get or when it would stop, or if I would survive. I was doubting my ability to give birth to this baby, to care for her, to keep her alive and raise her to adulthood.

On my retreats with Anagarika I acquired certain emotional tools that brought comfort during this time of doubting. Foremost among them was the skill of letting go. As a woman growing up in a Western culture I was expected to be in control most of the time. Many things require control, but it is not good training for pregnancy. When I try to maintain the illusion that I am in control, I am working against Nature. When I am working with Nature, I watch, listen, and respond. By letting go, I reach a state of receptivity, of *not knowing,* that does not require plans because each moment brings with it an intuitive response. When I let go and trust life's flow, I can relax and listen to the wisdom of each moment.

When I was pregnant the differences between each unique moment became marked and easy to read. My body insisted that I lie down, that I eat certain foods, that I move in new ways. In order to flow with the changes my body was going through, I needed to listen, to pay attention. When I failed to listen to my body it would torment me until I did. Messages I could ignore before I was pregnant, such as "It's time to eat" or "It's time to rest," were more explicit and had greater consequences when ignored. Messages such as "Get off that couch and have something

BUDDHA MOM

to eat now or you will feel so sick you'll want to puke" were ab-
solutely clear.

The life force, the power of Nature, became a part of my
everyday awareness when I was pregnant. When I turned away
from the outside world and focused inward, the veils of Isis, the
Egyptian goddess of heaven and earth, were temporarily lifted,
revealing the mysteries of life re-creating itself. Much later, after
the force of Nature had fulfilled its mission through me, that veil
was lowered again but never forgotten. I experienced the life force
in subtler ways at each menses, but while I was pregnant, the life
force stretched and danced in my body with abandon. Life was no
longer something to be gazed at as a spectator gazes at a thunder-
storm. I was in the eye of the storm, and depending upon my relationship to my body and my relationship to my spiritual practice,
it was sometimes wondrous and sometimes horrifying. It was horrifying to feel something so powerful take over my body, to make
me nauseous with its dizzying speed. It was wondrous to feel a
part of all that is, to be so intimate with the life force that ani-
mates all things. As Sengstan, the third Zen patriarch, wrote,
"One thing, all things: move amoung [sic] and intermingle, without distraction. To live in this realization is to be without anxiety
about non-perfection."

During my pregnancy, maintaining a strong body was one
thing I could control, and I clung to it dearly. I ate well and
stopped a pack-a-day smoking habit. I was viscerally aware of how
cruel it was to force a trapped baby to suffer from the effects of
chemicals. I was inspired to stay cleaner and healthier than I had
ever been before. There was someone who needed me to take care
of myself, someone whose existence depended on my health. A
bond of love between my baby and me was already beginning to
form, and I expressed that love by caring for my body. I was

10

acutely aware of how self-love and the lack of it were already having an impact on my baby.

As I became more comfortable with my pregnancy and turned more inward, I felt protected even as I became more physically and emotionally vulnerable. In this state of vulnerability I avoided insensitive people and situations as much as possible. Dr. Sontag's research in prenatal development revealed that "[s]tresses which increase maternal neurohormonal production do heighten a child's biological susceptibility to emotional distress." In an attempt to protect myself I was driven, unknowingly, to protect my unborn child. Like Isadora Duncan, I found that "[p]eople said such banalities. How little is appreciated the sanctity of the pregnant mother." Being much more sensitive to toxic situations during pregnancy, I avoided them whenever possible. This was sometimes very difficult as it meant avoiding certain relatives and friends. When I'm on retreat I find myself getting more and more sensitive as my meditation deepens my awareness. Sometimes I don't always realize how sensitized I've become until after the retreat, when I return to the outer world and suddenly feel like a snail that has lost its shell.

Many cultures honor the sensitive state of pregnancy. In almost all tribal cultures pregnant women are protected from anything that might shock them, frighten them, or appear ugly. The pregnant woman becomes a vessel for her baby and for the pain and joy of the world around her. She is protected by the community so that the species may survive. She becomes a part of Nature, and if her life is harmonious she will be happy; if it is filled with tension and aggression, that tension and aggressiveness will seem amplified.

I sought peaceful contemplative environments whenever possible. During the seventh month of my pregnancy, I went on a

Vipassana meditation retreat. I sat, walked, stood, and lay down mindfully for seven days with my baby along for the ride. During that retreat Anagarika gave me free run of the kitchen. On retreats there usually is no eating between meals, since that would serve as a distraction from meditation. Anagarika, in her wisdom, allowed pregnancy to take precedence over the usual retreat rules. The calm created by the support of my teacher, the community, and the meditation practice was shared with the baby inside me.

At one point we were doing a meditation practice that had us focus on the arising and falling of both *nama* (consciousness), and *rupa* (materiality). In Vipassana meditation, one contemplates the changing nature of both matter and thoughts. We see the arising and passing of the physical world by observing how everything we can experience with our senses comes into being, has its life, and then passes. The same is true for thoughts. They come into being, have their life, and then pass. As I practiced this meditation on the arising and passing of both matter and mind, I became aware that there was a *nama* in my *rupa,* a mind in my matter! Pregnancy is the only time a person has another's consciousness actually within her body. It is the closest two beings can ever be— a great responsibility and privilege. The retreat was richly enhanced by my pregnancy and vice versa.

During pregnancy mother and baby are physically and emotionally linked through the mother's blood, which carries nutrients and toxins as well as hormones to the baby through the placenta. It is through these hormones that the baby is viscerally affected by its mother's emotions. Fear creates adrenaline; well-being creates natural tranquilizers. The baby within the womb is an extremely sensitive being. Dr. Verny, in his book *The Secret Life of the Unborn Child,* writes that Dr. Albert Liley and Dr. Margaret Liley "at last provided what had been so sorely lacking, hard, incontestable physiological evidence that the fetus is a hearing, sensing, feeling being."

The baby within a woman's womb responds directly to whatever she ingests as well as to her emotional states via the hormones triggered by her emotions. She makes a lasting impression on her child's life by her thoughts and feelings during pregnancy. The more beautiful and loving the pregnant woman's thoughts and feelings, the more the child is nurtured. As a meditator I was able to watch my thoughts and weed out the negative ones. Like a gardener I replaced the weeds with beautiful plants and then watered the thought plants with loving affirmations. The fact that my thoughts were affecting my unborn child gave the practice more focus and fire.

It is important to remember, however, that pregnant women are bound to have a full spectrum of thoughts and feelings and stresses just as everyone else and that the unborn baby is surprisingly resilient. The most important aspect of a baby's experience is its mother's self-love. When I can simply regard my thoughts and feelings without being judgmental, as I do in meditation, those thoughts can pass through me without leaving a sticky residue or gaining power. Life is not always harmonious, and babies, like adults, are well equipped to deal with that fact. During pregnancy I realized how important it was to live each moment of my life, as much as possible, in a state of meditation. Each moment affected the precious life within me.

By the ninth month I was drawn so far inward that I felt as though I were brushing up against my core. I folded myself snugly within the cocoon I had created in order to nurture myself and the life within me. I didn't want to travel or move far from my home. My home became a sacred temple, and I became the goddess Hestia rekindling the hearth. I cleaned and moved furniture around and painted and made curtains. I quilted and made the baby's bassinet sweet and inviting. Each morning I would make sure everything in the house was fresh, clean, and ready for the holy stranger that could come at any moment. Women throughout the world have felt this holiness in the last weeks of pregnancy. Cleanliness and order became more important than ever. Dishes in the sink that previously would have gone unnoticed now demanded my immediate attention.

Pregnancy is both like and unlike sloth. Although I had an inclination to rest, it was an active state of rest; there was constant activity within. I was growing in consciousness at a natural effortless pace. As the time to give birth drew near, my cocoon started feeling tight and constricted. I felt the hindrance of restlessness and became impatient to break out of this tightness and birth the child. How often, just before a breakthrough on retreat, had I felt this same restlessness. Right before breakthroughs into deeper tranquillity I had a powerful urge to get off my pillow. Discomfort inevitably sets in before I am willing to make a major change. The discomfort I experienced provided me with the will to change; otherwise I might have been content to remain the same. The Buddha taught that to be born into the human realm is even a greater blessing than to be born into heavenly realms because in the human form there is both pain and pleasure spurring us on toward enlightenment. The discomfort of that last month of pregnancy helped me leave behind the sensuality of pregnancy for the more challenging stages of birthing and early motherhood.

As my pregnancy progressed, the turning inward I was charged with was creating more and more distance between my husband and me. It is not uncommon for the father to feel left out during this important transition. He is suddenly faced with the responsibility of protecting and supporting a family and may fear the loss of personal freedom. For a man who has been free and independent all his life, the pregnancy of his mate may be a tremendous jolt. The man who views his life as a path to deeper spiritual insight may feel a desire to bolt and run yet make the higher choice to stay and grow. He stays with his mate as she turns inward and may not be as available to him. This too is preparation for how it will be when the mother is fully engaged in the care and well-being of her tiny charge.

Pregnancy can be a time of conflict for a couple. Pregnancy can also be a time of great bonding if the man is willing to take a supportive role, rather than that of the main character. Childbirth is an arena where the woman will take the lead and will hopefully become a gentle, patient teacher. If a man is willing to surrender his pride and become a student, he receives an opportunity to regain his long lost feminine aspects, to express unconditional love and tenderness, and to deepen connection to his spiritual nature.

One of the greatest gifts I received by using my spiritual practice to turn inward during pregnancy was a deeper sensitivity to the developing child within me. By listening with my inner ear I was able to get to know my baby before she was even born. During pregnancy I was laying the groundwork for the future relationship with my child. Margaret Mead wrote, "However, I could do something about anxieties . . . by disciplining myself not to expect the child to be any special kind of person of my own devising. I felt deeply—as I still feel—that this is the most important point about bringing into the world a child that will have its own unique and clear identity." A child's identity and self-esteem begin in the womb. Who she will become is a complete mystery. I awaited this child's arrival with joyful expectancy and, as much as possible, lay aside expectations.

I became particularly aware of my baby's unique identity while I was on the meditation retreat. As I was sitting in silent meditation, the baby moved around, yet there was a serenity and awareness about her. The depth of the serenity I felt coming from her inspired me to give her the middle name Serena. To this day I am struck by her still serene nature and her high level of awareness. Even in the womb my baby's personality made itself known to me whenever I listened quietly.

During pregnancy I was pulled to the earth. I became part of Nature, a vehicle for life's perpetuation of itself. My body became a holy sanctuary in which the magic of new life was unfolding. I was serving humanity by sacrificing my body for humanity's re-creation as I took part in creating the next generation. Just as we feed and clothe our priests and holy men and women as they turn inward to gain insights that serve us, we need to protect and care for the inward-turning pregnant woman. By surrounding her with love and protection we support her in loving her unborn child.

BIRTHING

Initiation

> In those depths we are given a sense of the one cosmic power;
> there we are moved, and taught through the intensity of our af-
> fects that there is a living balance process. On those levels the
> conscious ego is overwhelmed by passion and numinous images.
> And, though shaken, even, destroyed as we knew ourselves we are
> re-coalesced in a new pattern and spewed back into ordinary life.
>
> SYLVIA BRINTON PERERA,
> *Descent to the Goddess*

As pregnancy turned my attention inward, preparing me
for birth, I was drawn to the wisdom of the women who
lived close to Nature and in harmony with their earth-grounded
intuitive selves. Just as Buddhism holds precious jewels of wisdom
about love and being in the moment, traditional cultures hold precious jewels of wisdom about the feminine arts of birthing and
initiation into womanhood.

In the solitude of my body I experienced the mystery of birth,
knowledge of which comes only through experience. With this
knowledge came the realization that in modern society we have
come to fear the power, beauty, and sacredness of the birthing initiation. As a woman living in the Western industrialized world I
had viewed myself as being apart from Nature. I had been taught

to think rationally rather than to feel intuitively. The model I grew up with was one of struggling to control the birthing process, using information and preparation to ward off the unknown. I came to realize that birthing would require a surrender of control and the willingness to ride the wave of the unknown with abandon. Birthing challenged me to release my imagined control and regain my natural, in-the-moment, free-falling awareness. The challenge of letting go to enter this nebulous danger-filled unknown was difficult for me. Thankfully, the beauty of enlightenment is that anything natural or unnatural, positive or negative, is grounds for enlightenment, and difficulties, the more demanding the better, are the richest ground of all. Giving birth was the most difficult thing I have ever done and one of the most enlightening.

I prepared for birthing the same way many other women of my generation prepared, mostly by reading everything I could find on the subject. But the wildness of Nature dismisses that kind of preparation just as a fire consumes a dead dry leaf and continues on its way. I soon discovered that all this preparation for birthing was making me anxious. The only activity that eased my anxiety was returning to my natural sexuality, my feeling self, my surrendering self: feeling the sun on my naked belly, enjoying the kisses and caresses of my mate, sitting with a silent mind, sleeping easily like a cat, wearing loose clothing, washing the dishes mindfully, listening to my dreams. These everyday pleasures helped to bring me back to my center. This centering lifted my feelings of anxiety and made it easier for me to relinquish imagined control. Pregnancy and birthing became profound initiations into my femininity when I was willing to become vulnerable and open to their deepest mysteries.

I was at home alone the night the birthing pains started. Jerry was away teaching an evening class, so I called him on the phone.

"This is it!" He rushed home, packed me into his new two-seater sports car, and we sped off to the hospital. My heart's desire had been a home birth, but since Jerry wasn't comfortable with that, we decided on the birthing room at a local hospital. I was scared, uptight, and didn't feel supported by my surroundings or the strangers around me. All the fears, all the unfinished things in my psyche were rising up to haunt me. I was afraid of what mean and dreadful things might come out of my mouth, what horrible monstrous movements my body might express. All the civilized expressions of my mind and body were losing the battle for control. I did not feel up to this task, yet there was no way out except to go through it, but through what?

When we entered the hospital I was told to register and start signing papers. The bureaucracy, the sterile white walls, the unfamiliar sights and sounds of sickness all around me, and having just traveled threw me into a spin. I felt like a wolf with its foot caught in a trap, frantically seeking escape, raging with fear at the intense pain I was feeling. Stuck in a strange room with strange nurses coming in and out, I didn't feel safe in the hospital.

In many tribal societies women give birth out in Nature, close to water. They squat by a tree, using the branches to hold them up and balance them. What a contrast that is to the white institution with beds and equipment and papers to sign.

Women traditionally gave birth in a squatting position. It was not until the mid–seventeenth century, when King Louis IX had his mistress give birth lying down so that he could watch the birth from behind a curtain, that birthing became something women did in bed. When a woman is sitting up while birthing, she is empowered; when she is prone, birth happens to her, and she becomes dependent on the intrusive involvement of others. Moreover with upright birthing the pelvic opening through which the baby must pass is at its widest and shortest and allows gravity to aid in the birthing process. When a woman lies down, the weight of the baby and placenta rest on the large blood vessels that run by the spine, which diminishes the baby's supply of blood. In the modern world, the birthing position has played an important role in the disempowerment of women.

I had chosen the Bradley approach to birthing which teaches the birthing mother to focus on the contractions rather than on an object outside herself. I had been meditating for three years before giving birth, so I was well acquainted with the process of following my breath. In Vipassana meditation whatever is most powerful to the consciousness in the moment becomes the meditation object. There was no doubt that the birth pains were the strongest object in my consciousness, and so I focused on them. I felt them, felt my resistance, and, as much as I could, relaxed around each new contraction. Jerry was my touchstone. He reminded me to breathe and bit by bit I reentered my body and began to release myself into the waves of contractions.

As the birthing process progressed, the insights of my spiritual retreats came to the fore. I was reminded that the creation of the new involves the destruction of the old and that the bliss of wisdom is preceded by the suffering of ignorance. The suffering that ignorance brings was pushing me toward insight. The process of birthing, like most initiations, involves pain. The pain was not caused by my being "bad" but by the changing and shifting that growing necessitates. Through the process of giving birth I was growing. I felt my consciousness becoming too large for its formerly comfortable container. Like a tree root breaking up the pavement in order to expand, the birthing was breaking me open. I could not deny the pain of birthing, finding it much more useful to face the pain and embrace it as an aspect of the initiation. When I tried to deny the pain, I interrupted the flow and created, through my resistance, more pain. When I accepted the pain, surrendering myself to the process, the pain became more bearable and the wisdom of the moment more accessible.

I encountered the natural human tendency to resist pain and contract around it. I remembered lessons from Vipassana meditation to consciously relax into the pain, to open to the pain. Focusing on pain may sound unthinkable. Actually, pain is one of the greatest meditation objects there is because it is so insistent. Its insistent nature carried me more deeply into my experience of the moment. Whenever I feared the pain, the unpleasant sensations became rigidly locked inside my body. When I allowed myself to open and accept what was in the moment, without fear or judgment, and with a willingness to experience whatever arose, even the pain led me to bliss.

Anne Morrow Lindbergh wrote, "Go with the pain, let it take you, open your palms and your body to the pain. It comes in waves like a tide, and you must be open as a vessel lying on the beach, letting it fill you up and then, retreating, leaving you empty and clear . . . with a deep breath—it has to be as deep as the pain—one reaches a kind of inner freedom from pain, as though the pain were not yours but your body's. The spirit lays the body on the altar."

By relaxing into the pain, by accepting it and using it as a challenge to my capacity for awareness, birthing became an enlightenment experience for me. My mind became crystal clear during the birthing process, clearer than it has ever been before or since. I felt powerful, deeply sensual, profoundly loving, ready for whatever life would hand me, even death. I had let go of everything. I had maintained awareness over nineteen hours of painful contractions. I had gone through numerous stages from contracting around the pain and hating the pain to looking forward to the next contraction, the next opportunity to challenge my capacity for awareness.

Soon came the time of transition, with its more intense, seemingly unrelenting contractions. I was now in an altered state of consciousness from nineteen hours of meditation. My doctor still hadn't arrived. Nurses checking my dilation came and went, but no one stopped long enough for me to form a warm connection. I longed for the presence of other women who had lived through the birthing process and could support me with reassurance and peace of mind. I didn't feel safe birthing the baby by myself, even though Jerry was there with me, because neither of us felt confident about what we were doing.

In birthing, you should expect the unexpected. One thing is certain: The birthing process is powerfully affected by the emotional state of the mother-to-be. I was fully dilated when my contractions suddenly stopped. My contractions disappeared right after transition, which is unheard of. Usually at this time the urge to push the baby out increases in strength. I didn't feel safe pushing the baby out without the support of someone who knew about birthing, so my body, in its wisdom, bought me some time. Finally my doctor arrived. Fearing for the safety of the baby, he threatened me with Pitocin to get the contractions started again. I asked him to just give me a little more time. I concentrated on inviting the contractions back, and they started up again.

After twenty hours of labor I pushed my baby out. She was reluctant to leave, and I was reluctant to let go of her. Jerry cut the umbilical cord, and she was placed, wet and peaceful, on my chest. There was no hitting or crying, just the sweetness of my child, warm and safe against me. I felt a rush of bliss. I was a mother! I felt the most awesome responsibility for this soggy little person, this deep, profound being. I had managed to avoid taking any drugs during the birthing, so I had full presence of mind at this our first meeting.

She was not picture pink and cute but wrinkled and, in some mysterious way, ancient and complete, with her own personality. When I think about the first time I saw Nicole I am struck by how she is essentially the same person today that she was on that first day I saw her. She was, and is, profound, centered, very much aware of what is going on around her rather than off in a dream. They took a photograph of her when she was just an hour old in which you can see her little face studying the photographic equipment. I didn't assume that I knew her or that she was mine. I held her like a precious gift, like someone else's child entrusted to my care.

Nicole's birth was my initiation into womanhood. It was "[a] descent for the purpose of retrieving values long repressed, and of uniting above and below into a new pattern" (Sylvia Brinton Percra in *Descent to the Goddess*). I descended to the depths of my fears, reaching the limits of my endurance and my tolerance for pain. I brought back up from that dark region an awareness of my unity and commonality with all the women who lived before me and all the women who will live after me, from all nations, all religions, all colors, and all time. I had experienced the darkness, the depths to which a human is capable of descending, just as so many women before me had. I marveled at their, and now my, hard-won wisdom, a wisdom that cannot be expressed in words, a wisdom that can only be transmitted through actual experience. I could now see how futile my quest had been to know what birthing was like through books.

The one thing I regret was that there were no women at my birthing to hold my hand and support me through this initiation. A nineteenth-century midwife wrote: "There is a tender regard one woman bears to another and a natural sympathy in those that have gone thro' the pangs of childbearing; which, doubtless, occasions a compassion for those that labor under these circumstances, which no man can be a judge of." Women who have been previously initiated by their own birthings can help the initiate realize her new wisdom with grace and pride. Only a wise woman, one who had experienced the birthing process, could have quelled my fears.

How strange and sad it is that in our culture we have masculinized birthing even though men can have no firsthand experience of this process. We have brought it indoors, into institutions. We have devised all sorts of tools and instruments to "aid" the process. We have come to view it as a medical crisis rather than the natural, sexual, and organic act it truly is. Our bodies become ripe for pregnancy through the sexual occurrence of menses, we become impregnated by sexual intercourse and our sexuality continues to be expressed through giving birth. One cannot help but wonder how we ever got to the place of seeing birth as a time to "do" something, to intervene, rather than as a time to "be," a time to relax, to let go and trust. In most tribal societies men were not even allowed at the birthings. Birth was a female initiation shared with the pregnant woman's mother, aunts, and sisters. Even so the masculine gift of intervention during crisis has certainly been worthwhile: Cesarian sections and other medical interventions have saved many mothers and many babies. I am deeply grateful to the Western medical procedures that have saved so many of my sisters. Practitioners of this medicine are a blessing, but we need to honor a different process when the birthing can go forward as Nature intended.

Birth and death are intricately linked. A culture that is death phobic, such as ours, is also birth phobic. Joseph Campbell wrote: "Unless there is death there cannot be birth. The significance of that is that every generation has to die in order that the next generation can come. As soon as you beget or give birth to a child, you are the dead one. The child is the new life and you are simply the protector of that new life." Death, both metaphorically and literally, follows birth, just as birth follows death. Aztec women who died giving birth were honored in the same way as warriors who died in battle. In many species of animals the birth of the off-spring precedes the death of the mother. Metaphorically, when I gave birth, I died a child and was reborn a woman. I was no longer the one being nurtured; I was now the nurturer.

The reality of impermanence used to repulse me. I didn't want to think about death, especially in relation to birth. Yet all of Nature lives to regenerate itself; having fulfilled its usefulness, all life returns to the earth. I am one facet of Nature and am subject to Nature's laws. Prior to birthing I had been clinging to my youth; in giving birth I was initiated into my age. Though I lived through the initiation and continue to grow, a certain aspect of my youth and innocence died in the birthing room. In its place seeds of wisdom were planted. In an interview, Isabella Rossellini said, "When I had my daughter Elettra my body was an adult body of thirty-one. But I had some adolescence also. Childbirth took that away, and in a way I was very happy about that. There are no longer traits of virginity or the untouched. You immediately become a body that has lived, and I think there is a real beauty in that."

After giving birth I was tender. I had been shaken to my core, and, having no wise woman there to hold me and help me integrate these powerful new insights, all I felt was the death, the emptiness, and the loneliness of bearing these powerful changes without support. I was profoundly sad. On top of that I felt guilty because society was telling me that this was supposed to be a happy, wonderful time for me. My deepest feelings about this profound transition, from which I was still reeling, were not acknowledged, and I felt terribly alone with my own death and rebirth.

Just as a woman who has experienced giving birth could have helped guide me through the birthing, a woman who has experienced the transition from girl-child to woman-mother could have helped point out that my struggle had meaning and so could have helped relieve my loneliness. I share this now in order to pass it on to other women—that the strength of those who have experienced birthing can be as important as the skill of a medical practitioner. A wise woman can remind the initiate of the courage expressed in bringing forth this new life and help her by accepting, without judgment, all of the feelings that might arise. She can tell the initiate stories of how she and other women got through the rough times and what they learned. She can just be there for the new mother in loving silence. A baby is not merely a chubby pink cherub with no personality, and I was not just a happy little mother. Both mother and child had just undergone a profound and sometimes terrifying experience and needed both support and time to adjust emotionally, spiritually, and physically. It is my intention that these words help support the new mother in loving herself through these changes.

I was concentrating so deeply while giving birth that I didn't realize I had entered an altered state of consciousness, an experience with which I was familiar from meditation retreats. It was not until I encountered situations in which I previously had been less aware, that I realized how profoundly my consciousness had changed. I had become painfully tender and deeply compassionate. When I left that sacred birthing space and returned to the world of telephones and television, everything seemed different. I felt everything more intensely. Someone yelling at her or his child in the supermarket pierced my soul while a mother nuzzling her child filled my heart with warmth. I became one with the lives I brushed up against, and their pain became my pain, their joy became my joy. It's hard to explain an enlightenment experience without sounding sentimental. It's like trying to paint the glory of an autumn landscape without having it appear overdone and unrealistic.

Most women I've spoken to have told me there were things in their birthing experience they regretted. Each birthing presents different challenges, and it's easy for most of us in retrospect to find things we'd like to change about our birthing experiences. Birthing is unpredictable no matter how much we might plan for the event. It can hold all manner of surprises. Sometimes drugs are necessary. Sometimes surgery is needed. Sometimes there is trauma to the baby or the mother. Sometimes the baby comes before the mother is ready, and sometimes it seems to take forever. Very seldom is birth perfect. Like spiritual enlightenment, birth does not require perfect conditions, only the willingness to go with the flow and maintain awareness.

All cultural initiations—whether they involve hallucinogens, physical challenge, deprivation, or deep emotional and mental focus—explore varying modes of consciousness that ultimately unite previously disjointed aspects of the self. As an initiate descending into the darker regions of my psyche, I felt myself joined once again with my true nature and the universal principle—call it God, Unconditional Love, Cosmic Energy, or Spirit. Those places I fear, those places I'd rather avoid, those dark crevasses of the soul—they contain the precious jewels of wisdom. Those are the jewels I wore on my crown at my initiation from girlhood to womanhood.

As a birthing woman I left behind goal-directed thinking and entered an intuitive realm. Birthing shook me into remembering that I am a natural being. Even though I live in a world where the food I eat and the water I drink seems to come from the market rather than the field, a world in which I can travel three thousand miles in five hours, I am still a part of Nature, still governed by natural laws. Birthing shook me into remembering that I am one essential but small part of a force that is much more powerful than my personal will. It brought into focus the awareness that my own life, my own drama, is a drop of water in the ocean of Creation.

MOTHERING ✣

The Path of Loving Kindness

A child's development of both a healthy body and a healthy mind
in life is very much dependent upon the love and affection it receives from its mother. Likewise, speaking from the religious
point of view, if the mother happens to be a truly spiritual and
knowledgeable person, she can become a crucial influence in her
child's education as well. Therefore, both in the context of individual personal development and in society at large, the mother
is extremely precious.

HIS HOLINESS, THE FOURTEENTH DALAI LAMA

After giving birth to Nicole I began to see my own
mother in a new way. Rose was raised in Mount Vernon,
New York, by Russian-Jewish immigrant parents who were struggling to survive in a country where they did not speak the language or know the customs. Her father read Spinoza and the
Yiddish papers while her mother singlehandedly controlled the
household. Rose and her four siblings competed for their parents'
distracted attention. My mother got their attention by being *the
smart child* in an age when being smart was as much of a deficit as
it was an asset. She liked to tell me the story of the neighbor girl
who, apparently having a very active social life, counseled Rose

that if she wanted to attract boys she needed to "[s]top using all them big words."

My mother smelled fresh, like lilacs. She had dark brown hair, snow-white skin, and cornflower blue eyes that were windows into a rich and vital presence. She excelled at school, receiving a Phi Beta Kappa key from NYU and a master's in special education from USC. She loved to write. I remember her being happiest after returning from a session of writing lyrics. She would lose all track of time when she was collaborating with a composer on popular music. Writing lyrics was her bliss, but marriage and family became her central focus.

Rose poured all that brilliance and sparkle into being a mother, a wife, and a homemaker. Although she often told me that she didn't feel comfortable as a mother and homemaker, preferring the more predictable academic world, she approached her domestic roles with the same discipline and open inquiry. As a student, she could count on those As to tell her that she was indeed excellent. There were no As for mothering and homemaking, no awards or honors, and the challenges went on and on without semester breaks.

As a post-wedding present my father gave my mother a copy of *The Settlement Cookbook—The Way to a Man's Heart.* Her mother had claimed the kitchen as her own private domain, leaving Rose bereft of its riches, but NYU had neglected to teach her how to boil an egg. As time went on, Rose learned to infuse her cooking with the same intelligence she infused everything else she set her mind to. Despite her continued lack of confidence, she became a superlative homemaker and mother. She kept a beautiful, comfortable, and orderly home, full of light and health. Things just seemed to fall into place when she was around, lost items were found and dreams were given feet.

Above all, Rose loved children with a passion. Children healed in her presence. She poured forth her richness with unselfconscious abandon when she was with her children. When I say "her" children, I mean all children, not just my brothers and me. Rose deeply and authentically loved every child that she met, which made her a gifted teacher. People of all ages felt her unconditional love and would open up like little flowers in her presence. She never lost touch with the magical child within herself, and it radiated as joy through her eyes, her face, and her voice. It's not that she was perfect. She had many fears that ran her. She was competitive with other women, which included me, and she was often absorbed in her own world, rendering her emotionally unavailable. Yet, as time goes on my appreciation of her deepens.

Mothering is, above all, a path of loving kindness. The Buddhist teacher Thich Nhat Hanh writes: "Maternal love is our first taste of love, the origin of all feelings of love. Our mother is the teacher who first teaches us love, the most important subject in life." At the heart of mothering as a spiritual practice is the development and expansion of what the Buddha called the *wholesome roots of consciousness*: generosity, wisdom, and love. I was blessed with a great teacher in my mother. She taught me that the practice of letting go, the devotion to service, the development of the middle way, are all aspects of the mothering path.

Thich Nhat Hanh, who was raised in a small Vietnamese village, has been another great inspiration to me where mothering is concerned. He speaks of his mother as the most beloved goddess, as "ba huong banana of the highest quality, like the best nep mot sweet rice, the most delicious mia lau sugar cane." He honors mothering in ways that are foreign to many Americans. He points out that "[m]other is the foundation of all love. Many religious traditions recognize this and pay homage to a maternal figure, the

Virgin Mary, the goddess Kwon Yin." In mainstream Western culture we neglect this honoring of mother, the female aspect of God who sits as an equal alongside her husband, the father. The great Hindu lawgiver, Manu, declared that "the Gods are pleased where women are honored; where they are dishonored all works become fruitless."

Each mothering path is unique. Although I was carried in my mother's womb, many children come to the woman or man who will mother them through adoption. What an extraordinarily beautiful fusion it is when a woman's anguish over not being able to conceive meets a child's deep aching need for the love only a mother can give. However our children come to us, if we open our hearts wide to them, we receive the gifts of mothering.

Our children's characters are shaped by the person they spend most of their time with. A loving presence is required—whether it be the mother, the father, the grandparents, or any other adult caregiver—to teach our children love. Love is taught through actions, through example. It is a direct transmission. My mother would wake up at 5:30 in the morning to meditate and center herself before the rest of the family woke up. When I arose in the morning, the house was filled with the sweet scent of incense and a mother who was centered and happy to see me. When I was sick she was there to feed me soup, and she was there when I got home from school. She was my touchstone.

In school we learned about California history and algebra, but the art and science of mothering was not taught to students, most of whom would eventually end up struggling on their own as they became parents. The journey down my particular thorny path of parenting began by the stripping away of my ego in a most rude and unpleasant fashion. I remember going to parties when Nicole was a baby and having people ask me "What do you do?" When I said I was a mother I often got some variation of the response "Yes, but what do you *do?*"

In America mothering is not considered a valuable use of energy and creativity. It is viewed by most as an occupation with no status, no "sex appeal," and meager financial compensation and acknowledgment at best. I noticed a considerable difference in people's response to me when I said, "I'm a singer," or, "I am an author." All of a sudden I was somebody worth talking to.

In the fifties, when I was growing up, mothers were demonized by popular writers such as Philip Wylie, who wrote in his book *Generation of Vipers*: "I show her (mother) as she is—ridiculous, vain, vicious, a little mad. She is her own fault first of all and she is dangerous." As a result of Freudian psychology, mothers were deemed to be responsible for all their children's unhappiness. Women were offered models of health and normality such as *Ozzie and Harriet,* two-dimensional pictures of family life that were impossible for real humans to emulate. Moreover, Americans had achieved great material wealth and power and were determined to continue accumulating more. Couples moved far from their nuclear families to achieve this American dream, but many women, my mother included, felt isolated in their dream houses, like birds in gilded cages.

The fifties were dark times for mothers and homemakers. Pregnancy was an unattractive threat to the figure. Even healthy birthing was facilitated most often by male doctors, and breast feeding was still considered primitive and antisocial. In spite of it all, my mother loved her pregnancies, reveled in her newfound femininity. She even nursed her children, flying in the face of conventional wisdom. She, who had once been acknowledged for her academic brilliance, was now "just a housewife," a lowly, defamed, inconsequential woman in most people's eyes. This is the view of mothering and homemaking with which I and other baby boomers grew up.

Growing up in the fifties, being part of the "me" generation, I was trained to think in terms of personal and worldly achievement. Surrendering to motherhood wasn't easy. It required that I challenge the view that I had incorporated into my being. Whenever I was able to make this shift I discovered that my mothering became easier, richer, and more fulfilling, which made up for the "self" that was being sacrificed.

We revere our saints and holy people for their selflessness, their devotion to the well-being of others. A mother selflessly gives of her time and energy. Yet, even though a woman engaged in mothering may work selflessly all day and night, she does not receive the same respect that is bestowed upon those who work selflessly for humanity outside of the home. The Sufi master Hazrat Inayat Khan wrote: "To raise an infant, to look after it, to educate it, and to give oneself to its service is as much and as good as the work of an adept because an adept forgets himself in meditation and a mother forgets herself by giving her life to the child."

There is a sort of death that occurred when I became a mother. I gave up part of my ego so that my daughter could thrive. Being a mother takes considerable time, energy, and focus. I felt a sense of impending death during pregnancy, childbirth, and early mothering. I now realize that it wasn't physical death that I felt breathing down my neck. The death I felt was the death of certain aspects of my ego. To be the mother I wanted to be I needed to be less full of my "self" and thus more available to nurture another. I had to grow up. Selflessness in a culture that asks us to be self-full, is one of the central spiritual practices in which the modern mystic mother is engaged.

Mothering has taught me how to meet the needs of others, sometimes placing them over and above my own needs. I've learned to say "Okay. I give up this weekend to take care of my sick baby," without thinking of a reward. I wasn't taught to think like that in this culture. I was taught to think "What's in it for me? What am I going to get out of the situation?" rather than "This is the highest choice in the moment." These, to me, have been valuable spiritual teachings.

I receive unexpected gifts when I make the higher choice. Putting my own goals on hold opens up a space in my life for new perspectives. One woman wrote: "My children have encouraged me to allow time for watching, for taking pleasure in things as simple as the way the steam rises off a cup of tea in the morning or the way a good night's sleep can free the imagination to wander whatever roads it will."

Another spiritual practice we are engaged in as mothers is the process of self-inquiry. Whether we have made a habit of impatience, lack of discipline, selfishness, uncontrolled anger, addiction, or similar weakness, becoming a parent can bring those challenging issues to the forefront of our awareness.

Until I became a mother, I was able to cruise through life with very little self-discipline. Then the demands of preparing three meals a day, getting Nicole to school and to other activities on time, planning outings, and numerous other everyday realities, required that I redefine time and accountability. Every difficult thought and feeling that surfaced in my daily life became an opportunity to observe myself and to work on the parts that needed healing.

As a mother, I am engaged in the *practice* of loving kindness. This doesn't mean that I'm always loving and kind every moment of my life. To practice means to make mistakes, make corrections, try again, make mistakes, make corrections, and try again, over and over. Each time I go astray I forgive myself for not making the highest choice, understanding that I am a human being and am here to learn. Like so many other new mothers, I started on the path expecting to be unfailing, which made me vulnerable to feelings of discouragement and low self-worth each time I fell short of my own expectations. By starting with lofty ideals and expecting to realize them in practice because I understood intellectually how to be a mother, I became disappointed. Just as a mother looks on lovingly as her child learns to walk, falling down and getting up again and again, I needed to take that same loving approach toward myself as I stumbled over old habits and ingrained patterns. By seeing ideals as a path rather than a destination, I could relax and enjoy the journey. These all seem like such basic lessons, but how difficult it can be to put them into practice!

On the path of joyful mothering I've found the willingness to constantly forgive myself to be essential. Along the way I've made many mistakes, and I've often felt like I didn't know what I was doing. The ups and downs of learning are a natural aspect of development. I practice acknowledging my imperfections. Whenever I am able to accept that I am imperfect I can work on what I wish to change and do it with loving kindness toward myself.

When Nicole was six years old I took a workshop in parent effectiveness training with five other parents, all of us groping for guidance. We went around the room and introduced ourselves. One woman, with tears in her eyes, said, "I have two four-year-old twins, and I hate them. That's why I'm taking this class." I couldn't help but admire this woman who loved her sons enough to look squarely at her resentment and reach out for help. She was willing to admit that she had a problem, and she was willing to change. She was just an ordinary person like the rest of us who, from the depths of her heart, wanted to give her sons the best she had to give.

Unconscious mothering is worlds apart from conscious mothering. I found tremendous spiritual power in mothering when I approached it as a path toward further enlightenment. When I was unconscious, I naturally repeated what my parents taught me by their example—both healthy and unhealthy. As wonderful as my mother was, she did have her shortcomings, and I inherited both her strengths and her weaknesses. I watched myself teach Nicole that if she kept pushing she just might get her way. This was a pattern my mother had taught me by not setting clear boundaries with me. Nicole learned to give up when she was frustrated, and the family pattern was handed down. Repeating what my parents taught me is fine when I am perpetuating their virtues, but I get into trouble when I unconsciously echo their unskillful words and actions. When I am conscious, I choose which aspects of my earliest training I wish to emulate and which aspects I choose to change. As a path toward enlightenment, mothering has provided a direct route into my psyche and into the insights that have allowed me to make changes.

Becoming a parent has provided me with the opportunity to see the family blueprint that has been passed down through the generations. It has taught me that I can choose to make changes that affect future generations. Several friends have told me about finding themselves doing the very things they vowed they would never do to their children, things their parents did to them. I, too, have found my parents' words, both kind and cruel, coming out of my mouth many times. It always happens so quickly and so automatically. I act out of habit, and it takes a great deal of courage, insight, and work to change even the simplest habits, let alone habits that have been ingrained in me since I was born! That's enlightenment. Where the discomfort is, where the heat is—that's where the growth is most likely to occur.

One unexpected reward of conscious mothering is feeling contented and grounded. When I express love and generosity I feel relaxed and happy. Love creates more love, and I begin building a happy life. Even though my intention may not be to get love back, it still comes back to me. I literally create a loving world which I then inhabit. When I sit around and wait for love to come to me, my life can become bitter and sad. I realized how true it is that we are all responsible for our own happiness.

Hell and heaven are right here and now on earth, and the path to heaven is the path of loving kindness. Mothering made it clear to me that worldly power is useless unless we create a world of love around us. Nothing can take the place of love. When loving kindness is the foundation we give our children and the world, we are truly ambassadors for peace.

While engaged in the practice of conscious mothering I observe painful as well as beautiful aspects of my personality. If, when seeing the unpleasant aspects, I attempt to deny them, block them out, or try to make people think I have it all together, or if I hate myself for my problems, my work becomes unbearable and my suffering multiplied. When I was going through a divorce I tried to keep up the appearance that everything was fine when things in Nicole's and my life were really falling apart at the seams. The deception took a toll on my health and well-being. I now see it would have been wiser to let the outside look like the inside and ask for help.

Before I became a mother I didn't realize how much I would be learning from mothering. Before Nicole's birth I was certain that the skills of motherhood would be easily acquired. On top of all the cultural images of the "perfect" mother, I felt I must be perfect in all other aspects of my life as well. The *super-mom conspiracy* claims that a woman can run a home, raise her children, have a brilliant career, nurture an intimate relationship with a man, take wonderful care of her body and mind, and be ecstatically happy with everything in her life. It's the, I'm-going-to-have-everything-and-I'm-going-to-have-it-now syndrome: "I'm going to be the perfect mother. I'm going to be the first woman in the law firm. I'm going to have a perfect body and be a sexy lover with my mate. My children are going to have perfect childhoods, play Suzuki piano and excel in school and life. On top of that I'm going to do all this in a state of bliss." Trying to live up to these expectations grinds many of us down and leaves us with a sense that we are not really living our lives, not fully experiencing them. It's great to be well rounded, but it's unrealistic to expect ourselves to be *the best* at everything at all times. As a woman who left a lucrative career as a commodities trader to be a stay-at-home mom put it, "Having it all doesn't necessarily mean having it all at once. For me it means having a choice."

Many mothers feel they must always be producing, and feeling like they're not being productive can be difficult. But where children are concerned there is much to be said for embracing the feminine spiritual quality of just *being there*. This may require us to alter career goals for a time. Patience and a large overview of our lives helps to keep mothering in focus. There is no easy answer to the problem of juggling work and home for women who wish to engage in conscious mothering. It requires flexibility and creativity to find workable solutions to the many challenges that inevitably arise. Every woman needs to choose her own place between these two aspects of her life—work within and work outside the home.

I don't regret what I gave up in order to devote the bulk of my time and energy to raising my child. I always made it a priority to be there at 3:00 P.M., when she came home from school. Children grow up so fast. Childhood is so precious and their adolescence so vital! Children wean themselves from us bit by bit, returning a reshaped portion of our own psyches to us with each move they make out into the world. When children grow up and leave the home some women reenter the workforce. In the interim the experience of conscious mothering has brought them to a place of greater enlightenment. Whatever they do after returning to work, be it writing, politics, law, science, art, or teaching, or some other endeavor, they refresh and change that field with the insights gleaned from conscious mothering.

Some of my friends express the fear that if they became selfless as a result of mothering they might lose their identity. I've found it important to have clear boundaries, to know which were my needs and which were my child's needs. In this way I have always honored my own separate indentity. When I am without clear boundaries I become edgy and irritable. In order to love somebody in a healthy way I need to be able to clearly and soberly see who he or she is and who I am. That way I can respond appropriately to his or her needs and to my own. Rather than losing a sense of self, conscious mothering can help us find it.

The Buddha taught the importance of walking the middle path. It's a balancing act to walk the middle path between work outside the home and work within the home while mothering. We give ourselves totally to our children and yet remain individuals with our own unique destinies, forever letting go of our children in the process. There is always a silken thread between Nicole and me, but Nicole does not belong to me nor I to her. When I love Nicole wisely I bid her grow, and as she grows she leaves the nest. On the path of mothering, we are constantly challenged to bond and let go.

Mother Teresa said, "True love hurts, it always has to hurt." In committing to a lifetime of love I need to be willing to live with that ache. Mothering is bittersweet. When Nicole took each big step on her path toward independence, on her first day of school, her first apartment, a year abroad, I watched with tears of pride, of happiness, and of loss. Those times were both happy and sad. Our culture didn't teach me about these feelings. It taught me that I would fall in love and live happily ever after with my beloved and my children by my side. Whenever I fell under the spell of that fairy tale I felt the pain of believing that something was wrong with me, that I was doing something wrong. It was a great relief to realize that the fairy tale wasn't true. If I love somebody, his or her pain becomes my pain, and each inevitable separation breaks open my heart. Each time my heart is broken open it expands, becoming capable of more, deeper, love.

In *Mothering,* Elaine Heffner wrote: ". . . while staying in charge of her child's development, a mother learns to stay in charge of herself. She learns to see herself as an adult and to accept adult responsibilities. She develops independence of thought and the capacity to function as an effective force in the world beyond the nursery. She strengthens her understanding of human behavior and of the nature of human interactions. Strengthened in this way, she is well equipped to meet whichever of life's challenges await her. She is no longer a helpless child-mother. She is her own person and a mother."

The conscious mother becomes empowered. She grows up, develops understanding of herself and others, and develops skills that will be useful in the world as well as the home. The woman who chooses conscious mothering brings to her worldly endeavors, to her art, to her business dealings, a greater depth of understanding of people and a knowledge of how life unfolds. She learns to go beyond the surface and into the depths of the human condition. This can only be learned through direct experience and not through books alone.

I was led to believe that mothering was a side track on the path toward spiritual liberation, but that wasn't my experience. I have found mothering to be a direct path to spiritual insight. By applying my spiritual practice to the everyday work of mothering and homemaking I've discovered a road map through its tangled path and learned to value my feminine aspects. I've found that when basic spiritual principles are applied to everyday life, those values become real, alive with vitality! Ramprasad Sen, an Indian poet, writes: "What's so good in you that you deserve to be called mother?" We need to realize the true value of our work.

In China, a holy man was asked to write a blessing for the king at the birth of his first son. The holy man wrote: "Grandfather dies, father dies, son dies." The king was outraged and asked the meaning of this despicable blessing. The holy man explained, "It is a blessing when one generation succeeds another." There's a passing of the mantle from one generation to the next that is part of healthy human evolution. Too often we try to hang on to power, to sexuality, to the limelight, rather than pass it on to our children. Devoid of strong spiritual values we are apt to see our work and our vitality as our primary value. We may worry that as women, if we lose our sexual allure there is nothing left for us. Similarly, as a man loses his worldly power, he may ask, "What is left for me?" If material power is my highest value, then mothering and old age become painful obstacles to happiness.

I've had my share of physical charisma in this life. Now I look at my daughter, who becomes more beautiful each year, and I know that this mantle of physical beauty is being passed to her. I continue on my journey, knowing that never again, in this body, will I be ripe and sixteen. There are other treasures in my future, but that particular one is being passed on to another. I'm reminded of the Snow White fairy tale where the stepmother (God forbid it should be her real mother!) looks in the mirror each day and says, "Mirror, mirror on the wall, who's the fairest of them all?" The mirror always replies, "It is you." And then one day, when Snow White becomes an adolescent, the mirror replies, "Snow White is the fairest of them all!" One day we wake up and our daughters are blooming as we are aging. Fathers look at their sons beginning their journeys into the seemingly limitless world as the fathers are realizing the limits of theirs. This is the way of Nature. Everything is born, reaches a peak, declines, and dies. If we fully grasp the importance of these realizations, it cannot help but make an impact on our parenting.

Understanding the Divine flow of life makes sense of the sacrifice of mothering. I pass on to my child the best of what I have. I stand on the shoulders of my ancestors, each generation, hopefully, extending the reach of the previous one. I want Nicole to exceed my limitations. This is evolution. It is hard to pass the mantle to our children without developing a deep, spiritual knowing. If we know that there is something bigger and more powerful than material reality, then it is easier to give up the lesser for the greater.

I don't have a mother on this earth anymore. She died in my home after a long bout with Parkinson's. When she went into Chain-Stokes breathing, and her breathing became less regular, my brothers and I went into the room where she was lying. We called my father, and as soon as he entered the room, she took her last breath. Her ashes are buried under a willow tree in my backyard, and her lessons are buried in my heart. It is these lessons, along with those I've learned on my own mothering path, that I pass on to Nicole.

THE PRACTICE
on the PATH

HOUSEHOLDING

Fundamental Morality

Vacchagotta the Wanderer once asked the Buddha straightfor-
wardly whether there were laymen and women leading the family life, who followed his teaching successfully and attained to
high spiritual states. The Buddha categorically stated that there
were not one or two, not a hundred or two hundred, but many
more laymen and women leading the family life who followed
his teaching successfully and attained to high spiritual states.

WALPOLA RAHULA, *What the Buddha Taught*

When I came to a crossroads in my life, with mothering
and householding pointing in one direction and the
contemplative life in the other, I went to see my teacher and
sought her counsel. A layer of murky film had recently been
peeled from my consciousness, and I was enraptured by the beauty
and power of the spiritual life I was seeing. I wanted to live in that
light, peel off more and more layers, swim in the warm pool of
simply being. The rapture was broken by the sound of my
teacher's voice informing me, point blank, that if I was meant to
be a Buddhist nun I would be doing so now. She said that since I
was clearly engaged in the life of a householder, I would get the
most benefit from committing fully to that path. I longed for
what I imagined to be the intensity of a committed spiritual

lifestyle, thinking that the life of a mother and householder was full of distractions that would make attaining enlightened states more difficult. I wondered how I could continue polishing the mirror of my consciousness while dealing with the day-to-day distractions of a householder's life.

A spiritual aspirant chooses one of two paths: that of a monk or nun or that of a layperson, a householder. I wondered, What does it mean to be a householder with a deep spiritual practice? What does it look like when one is spiritually unfolding in the midst of worldly seductions? I knew it didn't look like the quiet life of the monks and nuns who are free to meditate often, free from the strong pull of attachment to husband and children, free from the pressure to make money. What guidance did the teachers have for us who chose to stay in the world and nurture the future generations?

Sometimes the most obvious, simplest answers are the most difficult ones to see. I was hoping to discover some exotic Tantric practice, something exciting and Oriental. In my youthful zeal I wanted to wear my spirituality like a banner, like a tattoo with "Born to be enlightened" in bright fuchsia print. What I found was far less exciting, and I wasn't thrilled at its sienna brown plainness. There, not wrapped in shiny gold foil but in a plain brown paper bag, were the five precepts, the simple Buddhist code of fundamental morality, agreed upon, to one degree or another, by most spiritual schools throughout the world.

The five precepts: not to kill, not to steal, not to speak unwisely, not to engage in sex that is hurtful, and not to take intoxicants. How simple! I thought. The five precepts plus the practice of generosity, loving kindness, and mindfulness—the straight and narrow path of the layperson. Nothing fancy, nothing exotic, just a lifelong tennis match between worldly desire and my higher self. "Good grief!" I whined. "Isn't there anything faster, easier, more exciting? Couldn't I just burn on through those layers of misconception to the blazing heart of truth?"

Throughout my life I have witnessed people taking the fundamental moral code and flogging one another mercilessly with it. It has been used as a tool of judgment. It has been used to control and manipulate people through guilt and shame: "Be good or else you'll go to hell." "If you don't follow these rules you are a disgraceful excuse for a human being." The amount of abuse that has been doled out in the name of morality is amazing. Is it any wonder that many of us, myself included, approach the realm of moral values with a bit of rebelliousness? We've all witnessed so much hypocrisy and judgment in the name of morality that morality hardly seems worth pursuing. The reasons for a moral code have been so distorted that it can even seem antithetical to spirituality—that's how thoroughly we've twisted this code of ethics by using it as a battering ram against one another!

Perfectionism is not spirituality. The sooner those two unlikely bedfellows got untangled, the sooner I could relax and get on with the work of evolution. Before I was receptive to using a moral code as a part of my spiritual practice I needed to exorcise this dark oozing shame and judgment from my consciousness. I needed to see that my mistaken actions and thoughts are not bad but human. I am here to grow and evolve, not to emerge each moment fully perfect in every respect. If humans were capable of perfection immediately upon hearing the guidelines, we would all grow wings and fly away en masse. I, for one, have seen no signs of wings sprouting on my back. It's a relief to accept the fact that I'm a fallible human being!

What a challenge it is to embrace the moral precepts without getting bent out of shape each time I falter and at the same time not make excuses for my transgressions. What maturity to say "Whoops, missed that one. I'll try to catch it next time." What softness, flexibility! What firmness, resolve! What self-control it takes to use the moral precepts as a tool for my own enlightenment and the well-being of my family rather than as a yardstick to judge others! When I became a mother I brought to the ethical challenge before me the added incentive of my commitment to give my child the best I possibly could.

In Buddhism, fundamental morality is defined by the five precepts. The five precepts are the five basic standards of thoughtfulness and kindness toward all beings. Through them I can help create a peaceful world in which there is safety and freedom for myself and those around me. At first glance the precepts—to be kind to others and respect the rights of others—look as if they were designed to benefit society. But at the heart of the matter the precepts are designed for the spiritual aspirant's well-being and enlightenment.

Morality took on a new meaning when I saw it as a route to my own happiness here and now. That others benefit from my practice of morality is an extra gift. The crux of the practice is to realize my own well-being. The goodness of one's practice emanates outward, reaching further as that practice deepens. It is through generosity, loving kindness, and the five precepts that I clear my mind of the debris that accumulates when I act out of anger, greed, or ignorance. By following this path of fundamental morality I am purifying my heart and mind. I am preparing for deeper insight and peace in the moment. The rewards of fundamental morality are to be reaped not only in the distant future, in the form of heaven or enlightenment, but also in the here and now. I get to enjoy the lightness of a clear conscience. I get to enjoy the freedom of a mind that is not bogged down by anger and yearning.

Being from the West I have learned morality from a God who

tells me, "Thou shalt not . . ." It is the voice of a parent speaking to a child. The parent is telling the child that she must do as commanded. At one point mankind may have needed a strong parental figure to tell it what to do. We are now evolved enough to choose morality rather than have a parental figure tell us that we must behave in a certain way. Choosing to follow a moral code is the next step in our evolution. In choosing, rather than doing what I'm told to do out of fear, I am honoring my capacity for making intelligent decisions regarding what is best for me. Although the commandments dictate and the precepts are chosen, they both promote the same fundamental values.

Choosing to follow an ethical code can be lonely and difficult at times. Following the precepts has sometimes put me at odds with much of the Western culture in which I live. My culture pays lip service to the value of moral conduct while endorsing greed, self-righteous anger, and fascination with the illusions of the world. Those who follow an ethical path will often be out of step with others around them. One only need look at the advertisements all around us to see where we place our attention, what we value. Those who choose that path become trailblazers practicing what they know to be true and thereby remaining true to themselves.

On April 5, 1991, under the guidance of Thich Nhat Hanh, I took the five precepts. In so doing I committed to a lifetime of deepening morality. I had taken the precepts before, on other retreats with other teachers. Although it has always been an inspiring experience, with Thich Nhat Hanh I felt a more profound understanding of the commitment I was making.

The first precept, as put forth by Thich Nhat Hanh, is: "Aware of the suffering caused by the destruction of life, I vow to cultivate compassion and learn ways to protect the lives of people, animals, and plants. I am determined not to kill, not to let others kill, and not to condone any act of killing in the world, in my thinking, and in my way of life."

It can get rather tricky when I try to define what "not killing" means. Does it simply mean not to kill humans? Does it mean not to kill unless someone is threatening my security or the security of my loved ones? To simply say "Thou shalt not kill" or "I take the precept not to kill" can seem rather vague. Buddhist teachers have been plagued with questions about this particular precept, questions like "What should I do if there are ants moving into my kitchen? Do I kill them? Do I usher them out?"

Very real soul searching takes place in my heart while wishing to be impeccable in my practice. I have spent hours ushering ants and spiders out of my kitchen, and I also have engaged in acts of mass ant genocide. In searching my soul for direction with the precept not to kill, I remember the advice of a wise teacher who said that the purpose of this precept is to eliminate hatred from one's heart. That is the work, and *not killing* is the natural result. If I have a mouse living in my home, and, even though I don't kill it, I still hate it, I am not doing myself any good. The hatred in my heart is still creating damage. Following the precepts is not simply about self-control; it is really about purification of the heart. It is for my own benefit that I refrain from hatefulness, and the mouse too reaps the rewards.

The precept not to kill is also aimed at removing ignorance from my mind. Killing can occur unconsciously, just as a drunk driver may kill someone without mal intent. The killing happens through neglect or lack of awareness. The precept not to kill advises me to be conscious and considerate in all my actions. It calls upon me to be a good steward of the planet and to care tenderly for all beings, to wish all beings the happiness I wish for myself and my loved ones.

Over time my understanding of the precept not to kill becomes subtler yet simpler to apply. It becomes second nature, as natural as breathing. I no longer need to puzzle over the intention of the precepts. The precept not to kill is not a hard and fast rule; it is a living, breathing process designed to bring us to the gates of enlightenment and to a deeper appreciation for the sancitity of all life.

The second pillar of fundamental morality is *not stealing*. Thich Nhat Hanh defines this precept in these words: "Possess nothing that should belong to others. Respect the property of others, but prevent others from enriching themselves from human suffering and the suffering of other species on earth." At first glance not stealing seems pretty basic and is an agreed upon value for most of us. Stealing conjures up images of armed robbery and shoplifting, the most primitive aspects of stealing. Our legal system mandates that if you are caught stealing you will be sentenced by a judge and probably go to jail. Almost everyone agrees that stealing is wrong, yet it is an intrinsic part of our culture.

On a more subtle level stealing also means taking more than my fair share, something that occurs frequently in America. We Americans monopolize more than our fair share of the world's resources. Built into our economic and social structure are gross inequities in terms of the distribution of wealth. Our society seems to have embraced another precept, that of the rich get richer and the poor get poorer. The laissez-faire Western attitude advises us, "May the best man win," rather than "How can we all get our needs met?" This too is a form of stealing, or greed consciousness. As a parent I see this in the subtle inclination to make sure that our own children get their needs met without regard for all the other children of the world.

In resolving to abstain from stealing I am resolving to clear greed from my heart and mind. The state of greed is an anxious state. It is like a bottomless pit that can never be filled. I remember watching Nicole and her cousins one Christmas. After they opened all their presents and played with them for a while, a sense of emptiness and dissapointment seemed to set in. There was a feeling of "What next?" No matter how much I acquire, there will always be something more that I want. But as we learn to peel away layers of greed, I want less and less, so there is less to make me unhappy or disappointed. And as I minimize my focus on acquisition, my heart is more open to giving to others. I become content to be where I am and can reap the joys of generosity and gratitude.

As I practice eliminating greed from my heart I begin to understand the meaning of heaven on earth. Just as Nicole used to play house for hours in a big empty refrigerator box, I am becoming more easily pleased. I become lighter and lighter each time I drop another piece of excess baggage. In not wanting I become more open and free to experience the present moment. This is the most immediate reward of practicing *not stealing*.

The third pillar of fundamental morality concerns our sexual conduct. According to Thich Nhat Hanh: "Sexual expression should not take place without love and commitment. Be fully aware of the suffering you may cause others as a result of your misconduct. To preserve the happiness of yourself and others, respect the rights and commitments of others." All societies have rules regarding such behavior. Some of the rules are designed to protect, and some are designed to control. I had to determine, for myself, what is intelligent, compassionate sexual conduct and use that as a model.

Partly as a reaction to the repressed Victorian traditions, sexual freedom exploded in the sixties. The pendulum swung from rigid and unnatural prohibitions to permissiveness and a destructive lack of any kind of sexual values. When moral rules are applied rigidly and without tenderness they can create outrageous sexual conduct. It isn't a comfortable approach to sex that leads to perversion, it is the combination of sex with fear and the concept of "evil." At the other end of the spectrum, I have seen a lack of sexual values create untold destruction in the form of unwanted pregnancies, sexually transmitted diseases, and loss of self-esteem.

Sexual misconduct can create immense pain for ourselves and others. Any sexual conduct that involves a person without his or her consent is an act of violence. If the two partners are not equal in their desire and conscious choice, sex has tremendous potential for destroying self-confidence and trust. It creates fear, and fear quickly extinquishes love.

One of the most painful forms of sexual misconduct is the abuse of children. When children are abused sexually their most fundamental boundaries are trespassed. They are left without boundaries, without a feeling of safety in the world. I have a friend who was sexually abused by her grandfather and didn't remember the incident until she was in her forties and in therapy. The abuse had adverse effects on all parts of her life. The pain and betrayal of sexual abuse is so enormous that memory often blots out the experience so that the child may survive in an unsafe environment.

Another form of sexual misconduct is breaking a commitment to be faithful to a sexual partner. The value of monogamy has been debated over and over. Is it a rigid rule imposed by others who are uptight and who want to control and contain us, or is it wise advice based on human nature? To answer this question each person needs to look deeply into his or her own heart, but once a commitment has been made, the decision has also been made. I, for one, am keenly aware of the value of honoring commitments made in a relationship. Only once in my life have I strayed from a committed relationship. Although I only strayed that one time, it destroyed a sweet relationship that had very good potential. I learned the value of monogamy from that transgression.

When I make a monogamous commitment to my beloved and then break it, I experience the disruption of my own mind in terms of my integrity. Whether the beloved is told or never finds out about the transgression is not the issue. If I am not an open book with my partner, I am holding on to secrets that destroy the true intimacy we could be sharing. If I do share the truth, I lose my credibility, since I have broken a solemn promise. It takes a great deal of time, love, and communication to rebuild that delicate trust. Such complication takes away from time I could be spending loving.

When I choose to be in a committed relationship I get to enjoy the mental rewards of trust, lack of jealousy, and the opportunity to be cherished and to cherish. When I commit to a spiritual path I am able to delve more deeply into its practices. When I commit to a mate I have the opportunity to become more deeply involved in that relationship and in my own unfolding nature in a safe and loving atmosphere.

When the passion of sexual desire has been ignited it is easy to forget that sex can lead to disease, create new life, and deeply bond sexual partners. I have found that passion without love or commitment leaves one or the other partner, or both, in a bed of pain when the heat cools off. Sex is best expressed in an atmosphere of love and trust and in the security of commitment. Then I can join my sexuality and spirituality in happiness and comfort. Sex becomes an expression of love and playfulness and once again my heart is light and unencumbered. My beloved and I both move closer to our radiant core through loving one another.

The fourth pillar of fundamental morality that is basic to both East and West concerns what comes out of our mouths. Words seem to flow out of my mouth effortlessly, especially when

I am angry, but how difficult it is to get them back in! Thich Nhat Hanh describes this precept in this way: "Do not say untruthful things. Do not spread news that you do not know to be certain. Do not criticize or condemn things that you are unsure of. Do not utter words that can cause division and hatred, that can create discord and cause the family or community to break. All efforts should be made to reconcile and resolve all conflicts."

In the Ten Commandments the Lord commands, "Thou shalt not bear false witness against thy neighbor." In Buddhism the precept is not to lie. Speaking truthfully is universally valued. How deeply truthful we are is a function of our development. The least developed practice of not lying is simply not spreading false stories about other people and things; the most evolved practice of not lying is opening one's mouth to speak only the truth. Most of us fall somewhere between these two extremes in our speech.

In Buddhism skillful speech is defined as speech that is true, helpful, and timely. I have learned to check in with myself when I am feeling a strong emotion and am about to say something. Is what I am about to say true? Do I know this for a fact or am I simply stating my opinion? Is what I am about to say kind? What am I feeling in my heart when I think this thought? Is there any residue of resentment or lashing out or subtle superiority or put-down? Is what I am about to say helpful? Or will it wound the person I'm speaking to? Is it designed to show how I am right or clever or better in some way, or is it meant to lift the person up? Is the speech timely? Are the people I am speaking to in a receptive place? Are they open to what I have to say or are their minds on something else? It's amazing how much I do not need to say when I follow this line of questioning before speaking. Ultimately all speaking becomes Dharma.

When I started experimenting with this practice I was in college. I decided that I would experiment with the practice of right speech for one week by staying out of all conversations that involved gossip. I watched with amazement as I became increasingly more isolated while others gaily chatted on. It was a powerful lesson on how rife with gossip so many conversations are. My experiment made me much more aware of how easy it is to use negative speech as a way to make ourselves feel important, to express our hostility, or simply to fill idle time. Each day that I follow this precept I gain more insight into the power of what comes out of my mouth, the effect on me as well as that on my listeners. Above all, this practice of silence allows us to see how rampant and socially acceptable unkind speech can be.

When studying assertiveness training I was taught to speak my mind. But just being honest is not necessarily the most effective way to communicate. Is the other person ready to hear what I have to say, or will I just be irritating her or him? What is my intent? Am I trying to prove that I am right, or am I truly wanting to communicate with the other person? If I truly want to communicate, I need the patience to find the most effective time and manner in which to share my thoughts.

Timing in speech is essential. There were times when Nicole came home from school and as she came through the door I confronted her on something we needed to straighten out. I didn't check to see how she was and whether or not she was in a receptive space. I invariably got frustrated at my inability to get through to her at such times. Communication is an art, and all art requires wise timing.

Whenever I picked Nicole up at school I would ask her how her day had gone. She usually just said something like "Fine," or sometimes I'd just get a grunt. Come bedtime, after a story and the lights were turned out, she often volunteered her feelings about how school had gone that day. It was her timing, not mine, that determined when this sharing took place. I couldn't force her to share before she was ready. Similarly I can't force others to receive my feedback, no matter how true and helpful it might be, if the time is not right for them.

Just because something is true doesn't mean that it's kind. What purpose does it serve to say to someone "You are neurotic!" It may be true, but what will be gained by saying this? Will the person say "Yes, you're right. I'll stop that right now." Will it ease my frustration at their behavior?

When I first became aware of the value of kind and timely speech I was stunned. I saw how easy it is for us to be unkind to each other without even knowing it. I saw how unkind so many of my own words and thoughts were. That was a painful realization. I knew I wanted to change my behavior, but I was afraid of being isolated and considered hypersensitive. My fears were well founded. The path of truth can be lonely sometimes. When I chose right speech I was lonely for a long time until I adjusted to a new way of being in the world. It took time to find a new set of friends who felt as I did. The Buddha said, "Assuredly let us praise the good fortune of having a companion: friends better than oneself or equal to oneself are to be associated with. If one does not obtain these then, enjoying only blameless things, one should wander solitary as a rhinoceros horn."

When I have others around who share my spiritual practice I find it so much easier to stay on course. After many years of relative isolation, I now have a wonderful group of friends who share my values. What a great blessing this is! When I get off track, my spiritual friends remind me of my higher values. The higher path is sometimes described as "swimming upstream." While all the rest of the fish are swimming along with the easiest choice, spiritual practitioners often find themselves going against the current as they put their values into practice.

I have found it valuable to have friends who are further along on the path than I am. They help light my way and give me hope that there is a higher way. This is the meaning of the Buddhist vow to take refuge in the Sangha, or group of like-minded aspirants. The Buddha saw himself as a spiritual friend. I no longer think of teachers as people who have achieved unattainable heights; they are simply my good friends. They support me, and I support them, by example and insight, to become happy, fulfilled people.

There is unkind speech, but there is also the lethal silent lie. Silent lies are the things we don't say that need to be said, the things that we keep from one another and that drive a wedge between us. When a parent quietly throws away a child's toy without talking to him or her about it, when one of the partners in a committed relationship has an affair and doesn't tell the other—these are the things that create separation and distrust and result in a lack of intimacy. Knowing the difference between a silent lie and a wise withholding can sometimes be difficult. It takes thoughtfulness and self-honesty to know when to speak and when to remain silent. Developing this sensitivity takes time. I've found that checking with my heart is a good way to tell when silence is better than speech. Wise speech leaves my heart feeling calm and clear.

Practicing wise speech refines the heart. At first I found the practice difficult, but the more I practiced, the easier it became. I found that words that used to trip lightly off my tongue now tasted sour. I now see how speech can be a weapon used to fend off real or imagined assaults and to strike out. By becoming more sensitive to others we begin to rid our hearts of anger and greed and become more aware and conscious. As we fine-tune our hearts we play a more joyful, free, and unencumbered melody.

The fifth and final precept concerns the use of intoxicants. This is the one precept that doesn't have a corresponding commandment. Of this precept Thich Nhat Hanh writes: "Do not use alcohol and other intoxicants. Be aware that your fine body has been transmitted to you by several previous generations and your parents. Destroying your body with alcohol and other intoxicants is to betray your ancestors and your parents and also to betray the future generations." Much has been said about intoxicants, and much of what has been said is more moralistic than realistic. The best reason for avoiding drugs and alcohol is to maintain a clear, intelligent mind. If you are busy polishing the mirror of your consciousness, it hardly makes sense to spray a murky film of intoxicants over your awareness, thereby dulling your vision.

It is no accident that so many crimes, from sexual abuse to murder and robbery, are committed either under the influence of intoxicants or for the purpose of obtaining them. As a foster parent I have seen the damage that crack, alcohol, and other drugs can do to our babies. These babies are either wired and inconsolable or passive and uninterested in life. They can be lovingly nursed back to life in many cases, but there is often some organic damage that cannot be undone.

We are just waking up to the damaging effects of substance abuse on families and individuals. My friends who grew up in alcoholic families are now realizing the psychic damage they endured because of the erratic behavior of their parents. Children are keenly aware of their parents' state of consciousness. They are like sponges soaking up everything we teach them by the subtle messages we transmit.

I went on a camping trip with some friends and their children. I was impressed by how carefully these parents fed and cared for their children. In the evening we made a campfire and sat around it. One of my friends pulled out a joint and passed it around. The children had been playing nearby, and one of them fell down. Instead of going to the child, the mother tried to talk him into coming to her. Her response was more intellectual and less physical than it had been before she smoked the grass. I could see a change in her parenting and wondered how the child felt, getting a more distant response from his parent. I used to smoke grass regularly. At the time I was in a lot of emotional pain that I didn't want to feel. Smoking grass put me into my head and took me out of my heart. I knew when I became a mother that this wouldn't do.

It is common knowledge that drugs and alcohol damage both body and mind, and yet tens of millions of people continue to indulge in them. When I chose to abstain from intoxicants I became a lone wolf and realized how many social interactions depend on intoxicants.

Marijuana is to my generation what a cocktail was to adults in the fifties. Because it has become socially acceptable, few people are aware of the physical and emotional price we all pay for its use. When I came to a point where I needed all of my heart to fulfill the spiritual goals I had as a mother, I stopped smoking grass. I had to learn new ways to relax and relate to people. It was then that I started to attract friends who had bottomed out with drugs or alcohol and were committed to their recovery. I learned about AA and have since gone to many meetings. I am always moved when I go to the AA birthday meeting with my friend, who is twenty-two years sober. There, one person after another stands up to get a chip: one day sober, one week sober, one month sober, one year sober. I am inspired by recovering addicts who have the courage to face their demons and pull themselves up. I am impressed by the immense support this grass-roots group provides. These are my heroes. AA views drug and alcohol abuse as a spiritual crisis and treats the disease from a spiritual perspective.

I keep reminding myself that the precepts are not hard-and-fast rules but guidelines to use with honesty and candor. Moderation, the middle path, is also an important piece of the puzzle. A glass of wine with dinner, smoking grass for medicinal purposes, and so on, are all situations that challenge any hard-and-fast rules. It comes down to being honest with myself and nonjudgmental while holding a loving intent.

Choosing mothering as my spiritual path has been challenging. There are many lessons to be learned, and if I am not fully present and in my body, I am not able to learn my lessons well or pass the lessons on to my child.

The precepts are the stars by which I guide myself, and I am bound to feel lost in the clouds at times. I continue to work on their actualization amidst my successes and failures. I have had to be patient with myself, forgiving myself as I falter from my ideals again and again yet not defending, minimizing, or glossing over my transgressions.

It's hard to know what spiritual lessons another person is working on at any given time. It doesn't help my development to sit in judgment of how closely another person is following the precepts. I don't let the unskillful actions of others hurt me, nor do I attack them with the precepts. We are all seeking the truth in our own ways as we work out our particular puzzles.

I polish my mental mirror while driving my child to school, playing with my baby, and listening to my teenager. I am preparing myself for enlightenment. The five fundamental precepts provide a guide, a cloth I can use to wipe away delusion. By choosing to live a moral life, we create a happier society. At the same time such a course through life helps me develop my own happiness, lightness, and freedom, not for some other life or realm, but for the here and now. My conscience becomes clear; I need not leave a wake of pain behind me. I need not even bother looking behind me. If I am acting with genuine morality I leave behind me only gentle footprints in the landscape.

Our children learn more by how we are than by what we say. It is my intent that by following the precepts I will model the behavior I wish to teach Nicole. It is natural for a mother to wish the best for her child. By following the precepts I give Nicole a more present, more mindful, more powerful example of what is possible as a human being.

SIMPLICITY 🌿

Ease

And all the loveliest things there be,
Come simply, so, it seems to me.

EDNA ST. VINCENT MILLAY, "The Goose-Girl"

When Nicole was a small child and I gave her a gift, she would tear it open and play with the box and the ribbon, virtually ignoring the contents. With only a simple box to play with, she would let her imagination take flight. A more structured toy that did more of the work for her did not challenge her imagination in the same way. A friend of mine who had grown up during the depression mused about how happy his childhood had been. There had been no fancy music lessons or soccer camps, only the streets and friends and sticks to hit balls with and tin cans to play "kick the can" with. He and his friends had been free to play and create their own world. The gift of simplicity allows our children to be in the moment, the aim of all spiritual practice.

Ever since I can remember I have been enchanted by simple things. I recall walking down the street in a rain storm in the subdivision where I grew up. I was delighted to see leaves dancing down the street in swirls of water as it rushed along the cement gutter, its path diverted by every twig and stone. I watched in awe at the beauty and movement of Nature. In the summer, on hot, sunny southern California afternoons, my brother and I used to go to the vacant lot past our house and catch horned toads. When we caught one, I loved stroking his head and watching his slitted eyes close in bliss. Here was this prehistoric creature, with threatening points poking out all over his body, completely contented, like a baby kitten.

By the time I was eleven years old my life had somehow become more complex. When did I go from simple to complex? I know that in school I was shuffled quickly from one subject to another. I started running to catch up with myself. I was no longer walking, seeing the sights, smelling the smells along the way. I ran and ran until one day, many years later, I was so unhappy I did not want to run any longer. I remembered the leaves and the horned toads, and longed to return to that simplicity and ease. As a mother I watched Nicole go from enjoying simple things to getting tangled up in the complexities of school and society. My first reaction was to pull her out of the complexity of modern life, but each time I tried, life swept us back into mainstream culture again.

My favorite book when I was eleven was *The Little House on the Prairie* by Laura Ingalls Wilder. I was fascinated by the fact that Laura had only one needle to sew with. It was *her* needle. She took good care of that needle, knowing that if she lost it she could not continue her sewing. I had dozens of needles, and I couldn't summon up the least bit of interest for just one of them. In Laura's world there was so little that everything had meaning. Remembering Laura's life reminded me of earlier times, times when my own life seemed simpler. It is that simpler life I wished for Nicole.

I longed for simplicity all through my high school and college years. While longing for simplicity I somehow found myself addicted to complexity. The addiction to complexity cut me off from my senses, dulled painful feelings. I had become wise enough to know that there were unfriendly forces in the world but not wise enough to trust the goodness of the universe in spite of those forces. Complexity became a monster I created, and I fed that monster because I thought I needed to keep it alive in order to survive. Although I knew the pace was the monster's, not my own, I thought that if I kept up with things, someday I would outrun the beast and be happy. The race was clearly not making me happy in the present.

After many years of struggling to live the life I thought I was supposed to live I decided to try living the life I yearned for. My husband and I moved up to Sonoma County and bought a little house on a third of an acre. I had my first garden, started recycling, and taught singing at my home. I had taken the first steps toward simplicity and inner freedom. As time went on the journey turned me toward inner simplicity. Facing that same struggle when Nicole reached school age brought home to me how strong the pull of the dominant culture can be.

In Matthew 6:28, Jesus said, "And why take ye thought for raiment? Consider the lilies of the field, how they grow; they toil not, neither do they spin: and yet I say unto you, that even Solomon in all his glory was not arrayed like one of these." Slowly I let go of more and more things and people who I had once *thought* I needed but who I came to see were creating more stress than harmony in my life. As I let go of how I *should be* living and followed my inner urgings, I began to develop faith in the goodness and abundance of the universe. As I shaved away the excesses of life, I discovered that what really made me happy were the simplest things in life—a good meal, a moment of shared love, an unexpected breeze, a cat snuggling beside me. This became even clearer to me after giving birth to Nicole. Nursing her, watching her, receiving her first hug, hearing her first word—all were peak experiences, so simple yet so fulfilling. It was from that deep wisdom, the wisdom that there is plenty for everyone and that it doesn't require strain or stress to live in abundance, that I chose simplicity with confidence.

When life is simple it's easier to see how each thing is infused with its own unique history. I may remember fingering the handle and feeling the rough edges of an old cup that I have cared for as I had tea with my mother and finally got to tell her something I had been wanting to tell her for years. A year later I was drinking from that same cup the afternoon my friend told me she was pregnant. The cup unites these two moments in my life.

If I have hundreds of cups, one simple cup is not so intimate. Things and people lose their perceived value when there is an overwhelming quantity of them. It's as if the mind goes on overload and ceases to see the details. I find a few quality relationships that are intimate much more nourishing than dozens of less intimate acquaintances. Yet, when I'm simple inside, I can give myself fully to whomever and whatever is there.

Men and women all over America are waking up to find that their lives, though materially full, are spiritually empty, and they are wondering if their struggles have any meaning. The movement toward voluntary simplicity is driven by a return to basic values, to spending more time with our families, to the support of things such as home businesses and simplification of economic goals. Some adventurous souls among us leave or alter their complicated lifestyles and become pioneers on the frontier of living simply amid abundance. Some moves toward simplicity are large and dramatic, such as leaving the city or a high-powered career. Some moves are smaller and more gradual, like letting go of people and things that create clutter in our lives. After visiting an Amish community, Sue Bender came back to her home to find that "Housework hasn't changed, but my attitude toward the work has changed. Early each morning I squeeze fresh orange juice for my husband, clean off the surface where the juice has spilled, look around the kitchen, and take great pleasure seeing it sparkle. Then I go out for a long early-morning walk with a dearly beloved friend. I don't have to try to make these simple activities more interesting."

Simple things, like being home for Nicole when she returned from school, helped us bond. It is these small acts of love that I find to be the most profound and most effective. In order for me to be there for Nicole in this way I needed to simplify my life and my mind. It is the birthright of all of us to have free will and to make conscious choices about the shape of our lives. I chose to live with ease, in tune with Nature and with ample time to spend with Nicole. I courted a simpler lifestyle, which, for me, meant moving to the country, learning to recycle, and living close to the land. It meant letting go of a career as a singer on the road, which entailed being out at night, and embracing other avenues of income and outlets for my creativity. For me living simply also meant eliminating anything in my consciousness that got in the way of being in the present moment so that I could be there for Nicole, not only in body but also in consciousness.

Although at first I felt that I needed to move to the country to live more simply, I now see simplicity in a new light. Rather than an outer shift in lifestyle, simplicity and ease come from an inner shift. The outer follows easily on the heels of the inner realization, just as effect follows cause. The pioneers of simplicity have chosen their path knowing they would find a greater lightness of living through this choice. They have chosen simplicity knowing that they could also choose to have more money, more complex relationships, more things to do and have yet opting for the enjoyment of simple moments instead.

At the core of the Buddha's teachings are the four noble truths. The first of those truths is that life is *Dukka*. The word *dukka* is usually translated as "suffering," which has made many

Westerners view Buddhism as nihilistic. The best definition of *dukka* I've heard is given by Houston Smith, who defines it as "out of joint." Everything becomes more complex when we live our lives out of joint. The reason there is dukka, or suffering, from being out of joint, is because of craving, attachment, and addiction. It isn't desire that is the problem. The suffering is caused by attachment to desire. There is a way out of this cycle, and that is the way of the eightfold path. Through the eightfold path we simplify our lives and our thoughts, thereby bringing our consciousness back in joint.

Simplifying one's consciousness naturally leads one toward a lifestyle that takes into consideration the whole planet and its interdependence. In his book *Voluntary Simplicity,* Dwayne Elgin writes: "Simplicity of living, if deliberately chosen, implies a compassionate approach to life. It means that we are choosing to live our daily lives with some degree of conscious appreciation of the condition of the rest of the world." If my having dozens of pencils means that a young boy in Africa needs to share a half-used pencil with his neighbor, my heart impulse is to want to give my pencils to that young student. Those who are aware that the world is one nation alive with diversity practice voluntary simplicity. By living simply we honor that diversity while supporting our human bonds.

When thinking about voluntary simplicity, I need to remember that until I have something, I can't give it away. I had an art teacher who came to the realization that no amount of schooling could compare with the freshness of a child's vision. He taught me that learning to draw was unnecessary and even counterproductive. Yet he had studied drawing for years and was remarkably adept at rendering whatever he imagined. He had the skill, so he could let go of it and concentrate on his vision. I still needed to develop the skills before I could let go of them, just as voluntary simplicity often involves letting go of something already attained.

If those of us in positions of power don't simplify our lives voluntarily, as we use up the world's resources and as the wheel of karma turns, simplicity will be an imposition rather than a conscious choice. I would rather take the initiative to simplify. If simplicity is imposed on me, I'm likely to feel drained of power, weakened, angry, and depressed. By choosing simplicity I become empowered. It is a priority for me to pass on to Nicole both an intact earth and the value of earth stewardship. She is the next generation into whose hands this beautiful land and sea will be entrusted. It is my intention to model good stewardship for her, yet I am often being taught good stewardship from her. When we go into a store she is quick to refuse a bag whenever possible in order to be mindful of conserving natural resources. She has taught me to be more mindful of things such as this.

To be simple is to be honest, sincere, unaffected, unassuming, and unpretentious. To be simple is to be without any additions or modification, to be bare. To be just as I am without a mask, without a cluttered mind. When I do not feel confident in my goodness I feel like I need to justify my existence, to "be somebody doing something." When I feel confident in my own basic goodness I can be simple.

There are times during meditation when I alight on a simple state of mind. I experience bliss when my mind becomes bare, when I let go of all the agitation, plans, and past dialogues—all the complexities of trying to control my environment. I accept where I am. The more complex my thinking, the farther I wander from that simple blissful state of calm. In that state of bareness during meditation, it feels as if the sky is passing right through my head and body. There's nothing in my mind to hamper the movement of the air through it. When a bird sings, the sound is not outside nor is it inside my mind; it's everywhere. My mind is simple, receptive—no plans, no goals.

For me to get to that bare and simple place in meditation requires steady practice of mindfulness in the moment. When I'm reading Nicole a story and am able to let go of all other plans and schedules and worries, I can be with her in the magic of the story and share true intimacy. It's much simpler to be in the moment than to be thinking of the past or the future. The past and future are not real, so they make a perfect home for phantoms and hungry ghosts. Living in the past and the future is living in fantasy; living now is living in reality. Simplicity is not something to obtain; it's something to keep bringing to our awareness.

If I am simple and honest, when I complete an interaction, it's over, and I am free to go on to the next moment. I don't carry the interaction with me into the next moment. This is the very essence of simplicity: to be through with the moment when it's over and on to the next moment free of any carryover.

I need to work to obtain all the things that sustain life in my culture, but I do have choices about how I order my priorities. Nicole did not need the latest toys or designer tennis shoes. What I bought for Nicole was not as important as how I loved her. It would be a much more painful deprivation for Nicole to not get to spend time with me than to not have new skates for Christmas. I remember watching all my friends sending their children to camp and my not having the money to send Nicole. At first I felt sorry for myself and for her, but after I got over that I found a free scouting camp for children of single mothers. We went together and got to enjoy each other's company. Leo Bascaglia says of his family, "We were poor as all get out but I didn't know it. We laughed a lot, we cried a lot, we loved a lot." The joys of family are in being together and sharing whatever life is dishing out.

Life may be rich, with many exciting and wonderful facets,

yet simple. The number of facets doesn't always indicate complexity, though sometimes it can. Sometimes, as a mother, I have so many things going on at once, doing the laundry, paying the bills, getting Nicole to her appointments, getting to work, shopping for food, and on and on. When I'm able to do each thing with awareness, then I can bring simplicity to each moment, regardless of how many projects I need to complete. Some people work at their peak when they have four projects going; some work better just focusing on one. It's a matter of getting in touch with one's own rhythm and staying fully in each moment.

I was thinking about simplicity in art today as I was driving across the Golden Gate Bridge into San Francisco to meet a friend at the museum. Among the beautiful things about oriental art are its seemingly effortless visual harmony and simplicity. It is spacious art. Movement has meaning only in relation to stillness. Fullness has meaning only in relation to emptiness. To understand the meaning of the movement, the viewer needs to fill in the space with his or her own personal details to deeply experience the art. Rests in music, stillness in dance, empty space in art, unstated emotions in writing—all of these are as important as what is put in. Art is an expression of life. It expresses the archetypal experiences of our own lives and so speaks directly to our hearts. If it is simple and spacious it speaks the language of the heart.

There are empty spaces in parenting too, when we are just there with our families. We are reading a book while our child is drawing with crayons by the fire. Every once in a while we say a few words. That's important time, time when we're not really *doing* anything together, just being. Those simple moments can be some of the most profound.

I used to believe in the myth that happiness comes from material complexity. I created a complex lifestyle to support that misconception and then found myself unhappy in my relationships because I didn't have time to sit by the fire with loved ones and not say anything for a half hour. I had lost intimacy. I was able to find it again by letting go of extraneous thoughts and activities. I was able to find happiness in the simple moments of my life. Happiness does not come from what kind of table the family sits around but from the interaction that takes place at that table.

HOMEMAKING 🐟

Everyday Art

Stay, stay at home, my heart, and rest;
Home-keeping hearts are happiest.

HENRY WADSWORTH LONGFELLOW, "Song"

Surrounding myself with beauty, warmth, and order reminds me that life is good and rich with possibilities. It is an aspect of my spiritual practice that does not come from Buddhism or any other religion but from my mother, who taught it to me when I was living in the peaceful environment she created with her homemaking. It is an aspect of my spiritual practice that I share with Nicole by creating a peaceful, beautiful place to come home to.

There is a couple I have come to love whose homemaking always inspires me. When you walk through their front door you smell apples, or freshly baked bread, or oak logs burning in the fireplace. It's always different, although I've come to recognize patterns of smells in their home, patterns that reflect the seasons and the weather.

The air in their home is cool, refreshingly cool, not the cold of an abandoned house in winter but the healthy cool near a mountain stream. The big windows open to let the sun and air breathe through the home, just as the inhabitants have breathed life into every corner of this structure of walls.

The house is one big room with two bedrooms and a bathroom winging from the center. Everyone gathers in that one big room. The cook cooks, the children play and do homework, friends talk and watch TV.

Off in a corner of the room is an old fireplace with a woodburning stove inserted to provide heat more efficiently than the old brick fireplace once did. Everyone gathers around that old stove to warm their hands, and laugh, and be silent, and argue, and make up, and tell stories, and dreamily weave plans for the future. Sometimes Richard puts another log in the stove just to punctuate a thought and then pokes it to watch the embers rise and glow.

That big room is so simple, with its sofa facing the rocker and the big overstuffed chair, the chair that little Lisa, the youngest of the two children, likes to curl up in, falling asleep while the sofa engages in hushed discussion with the rocker.

There are always two or three blankets draped loosely over the arms, backs, bodies of the furniture. A red and green plaid blanket left by a nighttime reader, a fuzzy orange mohair blanket, a gift from Aunt Karen from her trip to Ireland, folded gracefully over the arm of the sofa.

Off to the left of the room is a round wooden table that always has a flower, seasonal fruit in a bowl, a sprig of something living at its center. The center of the table is the center of the room. It simply and elegantly inspires family and friends to breathe deeply and remember to notice small moments.

When you sit at the dining room table you look out on a small container garden. If it weren't for the background of cold, gray walls and tall buildings with their windows like tired, impersonal eyes, you wouldn't know you were in the city. The container garden gladdens your heart and offers relief from a harsher perspective.

Side by side the two realities stand—the city and the warm cozy cottage. Which is more real? They both seem to insist that the other is an illusion, but there they are, the gray walls and the red tomatoes with purple beans winding up trellises. And green! So many different greens! In all its radiant color the garden is like the repetition and variation of a musical line. It is such a pleasure to eat the green with eyes and then mouth, to see the roses inside on the table, and to enjoy the scent outside in the garden.

The kitchen is well used. The tools, well loved, are displayed on open shelves and hung from hooks off the cabinets. Everything is open to the viewer, just like Richard and Nancy, the homemakers who present themselves as they are, aesthetically sensitive and thoughtful. They see themselves as parts of a larger picture. They have their home, their oasis, but they do not ignore the dry, neglected areas of society outside their home and plot together to help create blooming in these pockets of neglect.

Richard and Nancy's thoughtfulness shows in their attentiveness to the trash. There are different containers for different kinds of trash: one for organic matter that goes into a compost bin Richard made out of an old trash can, another for burnable waste that is used in the stove, and still another one for tin, glass, and aluminum that is taken every other Sunday to the recycling center. What little that remains goes either to the Salvation Army, if it's reusable, or, lastly, to the city dump. When something gets thrown away in their home they are reminded of where this material comes from and think about where it will go.

The cleaning products they use are simple and biodegradable: some old recipes, some new, one good all-purpose cleaner that does not harm the earth, some apple cider vinegar, baking soda, a few rags. They are busy people and don't have time for a fussy home. But there is almost always order and beauty here, even when magazines are strewn on the table and the children's toys are in the middle of the floor. There is a basic sense of peace and cleanliness in a home that is not dependent on perfection for its beauty. The art on the walls speaks to an elevated perception, of a world that is larger and more constant than the occasional coloring book or broken crayon. The pictures and quilts on the walls are like giants who do not feel that misplaced sock under the rocker. Nancy's grandma made the quilt that covers the wall facing the stove. Many times I've rested my eyes on its blues and purples and oranges, every time discovering a new path through the maze of color.

This home is filled with bits and pieces of the lives of beloved friends and relatives. Like a portrait of their lives, the walls map out the special moments in their hearts, and their hearts move through their hands, which find their way into the handstitched pillows on the sofa, the ceramic vase Nancy made in Virginia one summer, the wooden molding around the bottom of the walls that Richard crafted with his brother's table saw, the bricks they laid out in concentric circles one winter before the children had come into their lives. Nancy and Richard have married their styles so harmoniously that unless you know them well you won't know that you are seeing two different styles compromising with one another.

How difficult the compromises were to achieve, yet how easy it appears! I have seen the home shift and moan and grow to let in each new element: the child, the grandma, the cat, the second child. Each time the home was thrown into a frenzy from which it eventually recovered, richer from the experience.

When I imagine their home and momentarily strip away the art and the quilts, the rickety old easy chair, the pots hanging from the ceiling, the rose in the middle of the table, or the friends around the table, I can see that what's left is not really worth much. Just a bunch of plasterboard walls and a funky old stove! Such is the magic of these homemakers who carry the fresh air and sunlight into their home.

Matisse wrote: "I strive for . . . a balanced pure, peaceful art without disturbances or worries: an art that soothes and calms the brain—rather similar to a comfortable armchair." Artful homemaking has the power to soothe the inhabitants as well as the passersby.

It has been my good fortune to visit many different homes. I've been blessed by the interiors of small apartments, old Victorians, farmhouses, and condominiums and have come to the conclusion that it isn't money or lack of money that is responsible for turning a house into a home. The common thread woven into the fabric of the warm inviting homes I have visited is the loving attention and creativity of the people who live there.

I believe that we are all artists. Some of us don't have confidence in our creativity because we've been told that we have no talent. In my years of teaching art I have learned that people need only a little encouragement to bring forth their inborn artistry. Our homes are perfect places for this. Here we can regain those lost parts of our selves and let the seeds of our creativity blossom.

The home is a place where women, throughout the ages, in every landscape on the planet, have expressed their creativity. Their creativity has been interwoven with the practical day-to-day necessities of life. Warmth was needed, so quilts were made from scraps, quilts that are as balanced in color and design as any painting. Food was necessary, so women devised ways to combine edible textures and colors, scents and flavors that tempt and delight the palate.

Every culture has its own way of expressing artfulness in the home. The oriental practice of feng shui is an art and healing form that uses interior and exterior spaces to open up and free the residents. A friend of mine who is a feng shui practitioner came to my home to help me heal the old pain left in my house after my divorce. The first thing she did was have me get rid of the clutter: old magazines, ratty furniture, and things I had been holding on to from the past. As we eliminated them and the room emptied out, so did my mind. I hadn't been aware of how much these old, useless things had tied me to the past. I slept differently that night, and in the morning I awoke to the exhilaration of limitless possibility in a space that was once filled with the painful past. We moved my furniture around, creating more space and better flow in my living room. Doing this created more space and flow in my consciousness as well. The pieces of my world began falling into place as more and more space opened up, and I felt greater harmony stream freely into my life. I now sit in my meditation chair and look at the clear, open living space I've created. It brings me peace.

My first step in any creative process is cleaning out everything that is superfluous, emptying out the *just so-so* to make way for the much-loved. I clean my floors, wash my carpet, put away the laundry, get rid of things I no longer use to make way for my imagination. My imagination thrives in a clean, open space. From there I can choose my home's colors and textures.

The colors and textures I surround myself with have a strong influence on both Nicole's and my state of mind. A bright red room is more warming and stimulating than a cool green room. Colorful textiles help to create a sensation of opulence. Bare wood floors create a sensation of simplicity. I choose colors and textures that are healing to my family and myself. Nicole's room was painted blue to soothe her. I painted my room apricot because I feel relaxed and sensual surrounded by that flesh tone. I've chosen colors that I love to come home to, to relax in, and to create in. My surroundings invite a mindfulness of Nature's beauty. I love to see

the blue-green walls and the golden wood floors when I open my
front door. They remind me that life remains beautiful even on
the difficult days.

Styles of interiors are as wondrously varied as their unique
builders. I've been in homes full of marvelous old pictures of relatives and lots of antique furniture. These homes are filled with
history and a sense of continuity. I've also been in homes that have
no references to the past, homes that are simple, clean reminders
that now is all there is. Both styles work; both express what the
residents need to be reminded of each day. Different homemakers
are nourished by different environments. My friend who feels cozy
surrounded by Victorian collectibles would feel empty in the
sparse Zen environment, and my friend who loves the tranquillity
of an uncluttered space would feel claustrophobic in Victorian
complexity. I'm the only one who knows what makes me happy. I
listen quietly to my inner needs and honor them by creating an
environment that reflects these inner needs. I empty myself of other
people's ideas of beauty and let my own unique vision emerge.

What a wonderful, big canvas the home is! It is art that
breathes and changes. It is environmental art that has a profound
effect on those who are subject to its influence. What makes a
house a home? Even if I, as an artist, apply my skill and imagination to the house, it may look beautiful but remain cold and un-
inviting. What turns an ordinary painting into a work of art? The
inclusion of love, mindfulness, and generosity. Only then is it
transformed from attractive to radiant. If I bring friends into my
home it becomes full and alive. If I pay attention to the details of
clean floors and crystal-clear windows, the overall beauty of my
home does not get lost in the dust and mold.

As a homemaker I love being engaged in the tasks of creating
and maintaining a home: cooking, cleaning, creating an inviting
environment, maintaining relationships with people in that envi-

ronment, and generally setting the tone. It is a multifaceted oc-cupation that calls upon the mother, the artist, the scientist, and the healer in me. The artist in me creates the visual environment; the mother and healer in me tends to the physical and mental health of the inhabitants; and the scientist in me strives to leave the earth's environment unpolluted and even richer for all the generations who shall follow.

As a homemaker I have a tremendous amount of power to help create a healthy planet. While practicing Buddha's eightfold path I naturally care about all life—not just human beings but all beings, animals, and plants. I am a mother not only to Nicole but also to all the children who live on this planet now and in the fu-ture. Leaving them a healthy planet is a great gift of love. I have many choices of products for the home, and each choice has an im-pact on the environment. It requires some initial research, but very quickly the act of choosing products that are kind to the en-vironment becomes easy. I love this blue-green planet that so gen-erously sustains me. Whenever possible I buy products that support industries I can believe in. I buy organic produce knowing that organic farming maintains healthy soil that will feed my great-great-grandchildren. I consider the health of this abundantly gen-erous planet when I buy my laundry detergent and cleaning products. Sometimes they cost more money, sometimes less, but it's a priority for me to use the power of choice in a wise and lov-ing way. As my spiritual development deepens I become more aware of everything around me. As I awaken to the preciousness of life I become more mindful of the importance of all my actions.

Some women would love to be homemakers but have no home. It is one of the greatest crises affecting the American fam-ily at this time. It is unconscionable that one out of four children is homeless in this richest nation in the world! At the time of my divorce I could have easily become a homeless single mother.

Thanks to family support I was able to hang on to my home and rebuild my life. I was very fortunate. As the extended family becomes more and more fragmented, fewer of us have family to rely on as a safety net during tough times. A divorce can shut a woman and her children out of their home and dump them heartlessly onto the streets. This is a serious problem requiring much creative thought and action. I think about families pooling their resources and living together in community. Homelessness is a community problem, not an individual problem. I would like to work with others to find a solution until every child, every person, in this country is settled in the safe haven of a home.

My home is a reflection of my inner life. Just as my inner life is in constant flux, so is my home. There are times I feel chaotic, times I feel peaceful, times I feel empty, lonely, full, closed, or open. My home is not a place for rigid perfection. When I try to maintain perfection in my home it becomes lifeless, a place where the inhabitants are not free to express themselves. A home needs to allow for humanness, for messes and cleanups, for spills and breakage. This flexibility is essential to conscious mothering. Before I had a baby it was easy to keep my home in picture-perfect order. When Nicole arrived, with all the demands of baby care, I was forced to let go of the nonessential in favor of the essential. My home started to have a much more lived-in look and, although most of my houseplants did not survive those first years, the rest of the house did manage to retain some semblance of order.

There is a Japanese legend about the sixteenth-century Zen master Rikyu. It is said that when he was a young student his teacher had him tend the garden. Rikyu cleaned and raked the garden until it was immaculate, but before presenting his work to his teacher he shook a cherry tree, scattering leaves and petals on the ground. Rikyu was to become a master of *wabi-sabi*, which is the art of finding beauty in imperfection. *Wabi* is translated as "the joy of the little monk in his wind-torn robe," or "to fill a monk's robe with a cool refreshing breeze." It is the quality of being in harmony with nature and one's surroundings, just the way they are—dry dead leaves and all. The word *sabi* takes this further. *Sabi* is the grandeur of solitude, the ability to love and live with the imperfections of nature. American Christian women deliberately sewed mistakes into their perfect quilts to remind them that humans are by definition imperfect. Only God is perfect. To work at producing perfect lawns with no weeds can lead to constriction in the mind. To learn to live and love with the imperfections of our gardens is a relaxed, happy way to live. To love ourselves and our children with our imperfections creates a happy home. All things are imperfect. All things are impermanent.

When I look into a home I see a state of consciousness being expressed. Life is filled with both chaos and order. Chaos tends toward disorder; order tends toward rigidity. Some of my friends and I rebelled against the rigidity of the perfect homes of the fifties. That rebellion can have its downside. I have a friend who spends precious time looking for things she has lost within the bowels of her disorganized home. I've seen her buy a tool only to find that she already has a half dozen duplicates of that same tool somewhere under one of the many piles in her home. Disorder masquerading as freedom is just as binding and destructive as perfectionism. When I enter a home so imbalanced that it is tilting toward chaos, I see a family that never sits down together for a meal, a place where dirt and acquired *stuff* collects in piles everywhere. There are no clear limits to make the children feel secure. The adults are vague and barely present in their bodies. When I enter a home where order has been taken to an extreme, I often find a showplace with couches no one dares sit in, where no one is allowed to live and move because they might upset the perfect order. Chaos and perfectionism are both extremes. Chaos is the extreme of flexibility, and perfectionism is the extreme of order. The spiritual challenge is to find the middle path. A chaotic style requires letting go of clutter and a perfectionistic style requires letting go of rigidity. This is where my home can be my teacher and healer when I have the courage to listen to it speak. Having a shadow self is nothing to be ashamed of; we all have taken human form and we all have places within us that we prefer to hide from the world and ourselves. No matter how we may try to hide our shadows they show up in our homes and in our families. By relaxing and being willing to view my shadow I learn how to gently bring Divine flow into all areas of my life.

My home is a work of art in progress. I have chosen mothering and homemaking as a priority in my life. I love to bake bread, cook soup, read to Nicole, and water my garden. It is my joy and I am called to do this, but not all women have the same calling. I am grateful that there are so many different women with so many different callings. If everybody wanted to do the same thing it would be a pretty lopsided world. I honor women who choose to bring their gifts out into the world. They too need a nest to return to at the end of the day. We all create our nest in our own way.

As a young adult I found that a great many of my peers viewed homemaking as an inferior occupation, full of drudgery and dullness, and beneath a woman's dignity. My friends and I saw our mothers powerlessly trapped in their kitchens, prisoners of their own homes. The homes were designed with kitchens that isolated the "housewife" from the rest of the family. We prayed for our mothers' release while plotting our own escape. Many of my friends escaped into the world of commerce, defiantly throwing away their mothers' aprons only to wake up one day and feel like they had lost a vital part of themselves. Though I'm grateful to the women who fought so that I can choose my occupation, I've also come to honor my choice of homemaking as a valid occupation.

My home is the temple in which I find peace and solace. It contains the surfaces, the shrines, on which I display what I value. Homemaking is an art, a science, and a spiritual practice for me, a fulfilling and endless source of joy. The family and home are the core from which society radiates. I am united with many other women who are revaluing our own mothering and homemaking. We have the power to create a nurturing environment for ourselves and our families, and these efforts support a healthy world.

NURTURANCE

Cooking with Love

nur·tur·ance *n.* warm and affectionate physical and emotional support and care.

The Random House Dictionary of the English Language

When I was fourteen years old and unhappily groping around for something solid and truthful, my mother brought me to my first formal spiritual teacher. Her name was Ina, and she was a religious science practitioner. Once a week my mom and I would drive over the hill to Hollywood. She would drop me off at Ina's apartment for my lessons on astral bodies, theosophy, and other esoteric spiritual subjects. Ina's lessons fed my mind and helped me see things in a new way, but what was most nourishing and what I remember in the greatest detail was the lunch Ina made for me. Ina's lunches were very simple, very small, and precious, and I would eat every single bite. Usually the lunch would consist of a piece of bread, buttered, covered with a slice of cucumber or tomato and some cheese. Ina put the sandwich under the broiler in her tiny kitchen and set the timer for three minutes. When the bell rang she took the sandwich out of the oven and garnished it with a pickle. I quietly awaited this sandwich with such eagerness you would think I hadn't eaten in days.

It was Ina's love that I was eating. I was eating the mindful way that she prepared the sandwich, the simplicity and moderation. I can't tell you the order of the astral bodies, but I will always remember how it felt to eat that sandwich. I learned many things in my afternoon lessons with Ina. I learned about the beauty of moderation and simplicity in a culture where there is such mindless consumption we have become blinded to the preciousness of the details of life. She taught me how actions, in this case preparing a meal, can sometimes go straight to the heart whereas words may merely skim the surface. When I became a mother these memories became even more important. They made me think about what I wished to say to Nicole about food and nurturance.

M. F. K. Fisher, in *The Art of Eating,* says, "There is a basic thoughtfulness, a searching for the kernel in the nut, the bite in honest bread, the slow savor in a baked wished-for apple. It is this thoughtfulness that we must hold to, in peace or war, if we may continue to eat to live." When I am oversaturated with anything in my life I find it difficult to remain mindful of the fact that I eat to live and more difficult to share that lesson with Nicole. Simplicity always makes me appreciate the small things in life. Ina taught me that not taking things for granted creates reverence. These are the lessons I wish to share with Nicole.

My first meal was warm sweet milk from my mother's breast. As I drank my mother's milk I felt her soft skin and smelled her familiar comforting fragrance. Her milk had the perfect composition of fat, sugar, and other nutrients for my growing body as well as antibodies to protect me from infection when I was so vulnerable. I learned to trust as I nursed at my mother's breast. My mother taught me love and reliability as she generously created my meal within her body.

I nursed Nicole for over a year. Nursing was painful at first. My baby sucked so hard that she tore my nipples open. I was committed to giving Nicole the best start I possibly could, and that meant nursing her. After much pain and frustration I admitted that I needed help and called the La Leche League. They showed me how to heal my nipples and the best way to hold my baby to avoid the problem I was having while nursing her. After a couple of months of pain at each nursing, my nipples healed, and the nursing experience became one of the most intimate, sweetest exchanges I've ever known. It was a rocky start, but I'm so grateful I hung in there and got to enjoy the warmth and connectedness of nursing my baby.

Milk was the last nourishment taken by the Buddha before sitting under the bodhi tree prior to his full enlightenment. The story goes that in his search for enlightenment the Buddha experimented with a number of austere forms of practice prescribed by the gurus of his time. He practiced self-mortification, denying the body food and sensual pleasure in an attempt to let go of his attachment to the physical body. In this dualistic frame of mind he considered the body a distraction, at cross purposes with the mind, a hindrance to enlightenment. He punished his body by holding his breath till near death, by staying out in the burning sun, and by eating once every other day. His once robust body became emaciated. One day he collapsed and was found by a shepherd who nursed him back to health. The Buddha, realizing the wisdom of the middle path, discontinued the practice of self-mortification and regained his vitality.

Anyone who has followed a spiritual path knows how easy it is to get so involved in the mental aspect of the spiritual practice that we neglect the physical. We forget that there is only one spiritual force, which takes an infinite number of forms, and that any appearance of duality is an illusion. Our bodies are also expressions of that one spiritual force. Since Nicole's birth I have come to realize that my body is Spirit in form, the Word made flesh. The miracle of birth enlightened me to the miracle of the human body, and I experienced a deep heartfelt desire to mindfully care for my own and Nicole's body with awe and awareness. We don't need to create duality or conflict in relation to our physical and spiritual needs, for they are nothing more nor less than different forms of the same energy.

In the neighborhood where the Buddha was building up his strength there lived a woman called Sujata. Sujata vowed that if she bore a son she would make a special food offering to the deity of the nearby banyan tree, a tree that was regarded with reverence in India at that time. She milked one hundred cows and fed fifty cows on this milk. Then she milked these fifty cows and fed twenty-five on this milk, and on and on until she was left with the milk of eight cows. She used this milk to make a rice dish and brought it to the banyan tree. There, under the tree, she found the beautiful golden-hued Buddha. Upon seeing him Sujata knew that this golden figure was Divine, and she offered him the milk-rice, saying, "Venerable Sir, whoever you may be, god or human, please accept this milk-rice, and may you achieve the goal to which you aspire." The Buddha ate the milk-rice, washed the bowl, and placed it in the water of the nearby river to float away, saying, "If today I am to attain full enlightenment, may this golden bowl swim upstream." It did, he did, and the rest is history.

Once Nicole was weaned, I nurtured her with food from the earth. Life outside the home can be tough and challenging. The spiritual warrior prepares herself and her family for these challenges. Helping Nicole be an effective spiritual warrior included fortifying her body so she could go into the world well grounded. Nicole had difficulty with low blood sugar. If I gave her a good breakfast before she went to school she was happier at school. She played and learned better. On the days that she didn't get a good breakfast she was more fragile, more sensitive to being hurt, and less able to focus, so that she didn't learn as well. A practical aspect of loving Nicole was making sure that her chemistry was well balanced before she went to school in the morning. Even if a child has a keen mind, great teachers, and a safe learning environment, a poor diet can have a negative effect on a child's self-esteem because lack of proper nutrients makes it difficult for her or him to function. When a child has difficulty concentrating at school the teacher doesn't know if the child's problem is one of chemistry or intelligence. It is natural for children to think they are just not smart enough when they have difficulty concentrating at school. How important it is for me to carefully nurture my loved ones in this stressful world! Taking into account her individual dietary needs, I am cooking for my child's unique body. It is a way of expressing love that is personal and specific, the kind of love we all need.

I bring my spiritual practice into the kitchen, which is the center of my home. In it I create meals that feed my family; my family then goes out into the community and impacts it. These vibrations reverberate, creating a domino effect. If I serve love in my kitchen, we carry that love into the world and thereby contribute to world peace. If I serve wisdom in my kitchen, I contribute to enlightenment. When Nicole wakes up to freshly squeezed orange juice and an orderly, peaceful kitchen she brings that nourishment out into the world with her.

The Buddha defined the wholesome and unwholesome roots of consciousness: The unwholesome roots are ignorance, greed, and anger. The wholesome roots are love, wisdom, and generosity. All of these roots are given and received through our cooking. They are literally transmitted through the food. It's not hard to see which root of consciousness is being expressed in each eating experience. There's no hiding from myself in the kitchen. My reflection is clearly imprinted in the food I prepare. As part of my spiritual practice I remind myself to be aware of the attitude I bring into the kitchen.

Being spaced out in the kitchen and feeding my family things that are thrown together without thought is feeding my family ignorance. Feeding a spouse who has a cholesterol problem an omelette fried in butter is feeding him or her ignorance in the form of ill health. We don't mean to be deliberately destructive, but it can harm him or her in the long run just the same. That's how ignorance works: It slowly erodes our happiness yet without malicious intent.

In my ignorance I have given Nicole sugar as a reward and then watched as she bounced off the walls and ultimately crashed. Our culture celebrates holidays with vast amounts of sugar. It is very difficult to avoid the seduction of sugar. When we are healthy, foods rich in sugar can be fun, but when we're not well, or if we eat an excessive amount of sugar, it can throw off our chemistry and contribute to disease. With sugar, as with all things, there are no hard-and-fast rules, only guidelines. It was an eye-opener for me to visit my parents when Kalu Rimpoche, a Tibetan master, presented my mother with a big box of chocolates. It taught me that a pure heart is more important than pure food.

I have a friend who is a wonderful cook and healer. He came over one day with a bunch of tomatoes from another friend's garden and made spaghetti sauce from scratch, with fresh corn and basil, tahini, and a tomato base. Nicole and I shared this warm, relaxed summer meal with our friend. When I sat down to eat I had not been feeling well. I had been having a hard day: Nicole and I had been at odds, and there were problems at work. But after this meal I felt more centered, more content. Nicole and I settled into a peaceful space with each other. My friend had fed us wisely.

Another root of consciousness that Buddha described is greed. It has its origin in feeling like there's not enough, a feeling that there's not enough food, love, or time. It's like desperately trying to fill a bottomless pit. Greed is created by the feeling that simply being is not good enough, that you have to do something to make your existence substantial.

Greed is created by a lack of trust. It happens when we're very young and dependent on caretakers who are not able to meet our basic needs. If I don't know how it feels to be satisfied, if I don't have an awareness of the abundance of life, I become like a hungry ghost. It doesn't matter how much I ingest; the nurturance just pours out of my vaporous body. When I have a sense of abundance I can take a tomato, slice it, put some basil on it, and it looks beautiful and tastes wonderful. Basil and tomato—simple, delicious!

Another way greed shows up in the kitchen is when a family doesn't feel like there is enough love to go around. When there's a trickle of love rather than a free flow, a child's body and spirit become emaciated. When children starve themselves, their physical bodies mirror their starving spiritual bodies.

On the other extreme, when one constantly tries to fill oneself up with something real, with love, but has to settle for its metaphor, food, the food pads and armors the hungry eater from the pain of the world. I watched myself one lonely day sitting in front of the TV. I kept going to the kitchen instead of calling a friend. I saw in my own attempt to fill loneliness with food that overeating and self-starvation can both be symptoms of loneliness. Being full is not the same as being satisfied. It's impossible to find honest loving contact in a cream pie. When I eat donuts or any food devoid of loving, caring contact, how can I possibly find satisfaction? In the meantime the donuts turn into useless fat deposits, cholesterol that lines the arteries and sugar that disrupts my body chemistry, making me more vulnerable to mood swings, irritability, fatigue, and restlessness.

Anger is the third unwholesome root of consciousness. Anger is sometimes expressed by habitually burning the meal. I have a friend whose mother was always feuding with his father. She made her meals like a *good wife* but they were often burnt offerings. When I sat down to a meal with my friend he talked about always walking away from his mother's table with a stomachache. Burning food and other forms of carelessness can be indirect and unconscious ways of expressing our anger. How easy it is to unconsciously take our anger out into the world!

There are many ways that a spiritual practice can inform our attitudes toward food. One way is by raising the question of whether or not to eat meat. The precept not to kill comes into play here, though there are many other sound reasons for choosing a meatless diet. A vegetarian diet is less expensive than one that includes meat. Ecologically, vegetarianism creates less stress on the environment since food that is grown is lower down on the food chain than meat and thereby uses less of the world's resources.

When Nicole and I drive down Highway 5 on our way to L.A. we pass a cattle ranch. The cows are all tightly jammed in together. There's no grass, no shade, no dignity or love in their lifestyle. I feel a deep sorrow when I see this. Nicole wanted to know why the animals were living without plants or space. Not long after that she became a vegetarian. The people raising these cattle do not relate to the animals as creatures of spirit. They become little more than dollars and cents regardless of the impact on the environment or what these poor creatures are experiencing. It is only a short jump to seeing human beings in a similar light.

However, being a vegetarian doesn't necessarily make one a kind person or a good mother, just as being a Christian or Buddhist or Hindu or Muslim doesn't necessarily make one a kind person. There does not seem to be a clear-cut answer to the morality of killing to eat. Native Americans honor the animals they hunt just as they honor the corn they grow. They express gratitude to those plants and animals, aware that "now we eat you just as you will eat us when we are dead and return to the earth." In that kind of reverent relationship there is respect for the animal and an understanding that we are all part of one spiritual body.

When I was suffering from malnutrition, because of self-denial and self-loathing, my teacher, Anagarika, made me some garlic soup with a meat base. I was struck by the fact that my teacher, who was a Buddhist nun, was preparing meat. Afterward we had many discussions about the precept of not killing and how it relates to eating meat. She said that karma is created by the intent and one can eat meat if there is no *mal intent.* Many Buddhists eat meat. I came out of the discussions with the realization that wisdom is not rigid but is about making the highest choice in any given situation.

Often vegetarians are confronted with the dilemma of how to make the highest choice when they are being served meat by a gracious host. At home I cook mostly vegetarian meals, but when I go to my friend's house and she lovingly prepares me a pot roast to nurture me, I eat the pot roast. Her love makes the pot roast holy. If I reject her meal I am rejecting her gift and depriving her of the opportunity to express her generosity. My teacher taught me the importance of receiveing gifts graciously. Receiving with an open heart is as important as giving with an open heart. Kindness toward my host takes precedence over not eating meat, except if there is a significant health issue involved. I feel that teaching Nicole about generous receiving is as important as teaching her about a mindful diet.

Whether you are a vegetarian or an omnivore, food can be a powerful agent for health. The healing comes from the nutritional value of the food as well as from how it is eaten. I find it so easy to eat to refuel rather than to nurture myself. Nicole and I sometimes forget to sit down for a meal together when we are running around to various activities at all different hours. We grab something to eat as we run out the door. We eat quickly over the sink or in the car. Quickness of preparation is becoming a priority in our culture. I wonder how this will impact our spiritual lives? I am bombarded with enticements to avoid spending time chopping vegetables and preparing meals from scratch. To do what instead? What is more creative, more sensual, and more important than cooking a beautiful meal for the people I love? It doesn't require spending hours preparing three meals each day but just allowing myself the pleasure of appreciating sweet yellow corn, nutty brown rice, and all the other gifts I receive while in this body.

Cooking and eating are two of the most wonderful sensual experiences our bodies provide. Being in a body is bittersweet, painful as well as pleasurable. Both the pain and the pleasure can be used for enlightenment. With mindful pleasure I delight in the colorful, fragrant fruits and vegetables and in the relaxed attitude of a cook who leaves the world behind her to play with the sweet, bitter, smooth, and crunchy tastes, textures, shapes, and smells of the ingredients.

There can be joy in the preparation of food, and there can be joy in sitting down for a meal with awareness. Sitting down at a beautiful table in front of a plate of attractively prepared food is a reminder of the earth's radiance and abundance. Placing a flower or twigs or leaves in the center of the table in a pleasing arrangement reflects what is going on outdoors and brings my family and guests back to their senses. The table becomes a shrine. In summer I delight in the orange, purples, yellows, and pinks, and in winter I'm grateful for each twig.

In the middle of my table is a lazy Susan. Sometimes Nicole will pick a bouquet for a centerpiece. Right now there are some red roses from my garden, red roses with a white crocheted doily underneath them and two brass candlesticks with white candles. Spread around the lazy Susan are artifacts from different adventures we've had. We have rocks from river trips, shells from the ocean, and various other things we picked up from our outdoor adventures. The children who come to visit love to pick them up and play with them. This table, where we receive our nourishment, also nourishes our senses even as the natural objects collected there remind us of the earth's many gifts.

My friend Denise sets a beautiful table for her three-year-old twins. She arranges child-sized portions artfully on a plate, mixing colors and balancing proteins, vegetables, and fun. She has a tiny vase with a little flower in it that she puts on their child-sized table. The portions are small so the children get a sense of completion at the end of the meal. Already her girls are learning dignity, moderation in eating, and the delight of stopping to appreciate the beauty that is all around.

Creating a beautiful table encourages me to take my time and appreciate the meal that is being served. These simple reminders don't require great amounts of time or money. They only require the desire to create a celebration out of simple everyday events. It becomes a way to honor our friends, our families, and ourselves.

In that aesthetic setting my guests and family are offered something real. Still, if the people I am feeding are totally unconscious, they may not be able to respond to my offering. As a host it is not my responsibility to enlighten my guests, only to provide an atmosphere in which they can be loved. I believe that after a while the kind, unconditional expression of love reaches even the densest of beings—although we may never witness it. The goal is to express love; whether or not it is received is out of our hands.

In Jewish culture there are many beautiful attitudes and rituals relating to food. In Edward Hoffman's book *The Way of Splendor* he says, "Here again the key idea is that we must make use of our higher intentionality, or 'Kavanah,' to exalt what is ordinarily a very mundane, even trivial activity. We are urged to eat slowly, tasting each morsel. Nor should we gulp what we drink. The meal itself would be surrounded in a calm and reverent atmosphere, and even prepared with loving attention. In this manner, by riveting our awareness fully on each facet of our senses, we can experience greater inner peace and physical health."

In the Jewish home, every Friday night is Sabbath. The mother cleans the house on Fridays to make it holy for this day. She sets a beautiful table, brings out special plates, and prepares her best meal. These kinds of weekly rituals realign a family with a higher purpose. We leave our everyday cares and concerns for an evening to unite with one another.

Some of my friends who are not comfortable with the traditions they grew up with are creating their own. Sharing a meal with friends and family helps me remember who I am and what I am doing on this planet. Special meals have become an important part of my family life. Through them my family reaffirms its vow to live together joyfully and harmoniously.

Mealtime is a perfect time to remember who I am and to feel grateful for what I have. I enjoy the ritual of saying grace or making a toast at the beginning a meal. Saying grace is a way of expressing my gratitude for sitting with friends or family and sharing a meal. When grace is infused with a spirit of genuine gratitude it regains its original dignity. Saying grace is one of the loveliest traditional rituals shared by many cultures and religions.

To express joy and thankfulness for the food that sustains us and the company that makes our journey worthwhile heals and affirms us.

The attitude with which I eat is another important aspect of how well I care for my child and myself. On Vipassana retreats I engage in the practice of mindful eating. When I eat my meal on a retreat I continue meditation by being aware of touching the spoon, raising the spoon to my lips, putting the food in my mouth, tasting the food, smelling the food, chewing, liking or disliking, swallowing, putting the spoon back down, and so on. I do this with each bite. There is no talking, no distractions. I remain aware of each moment of the eating process. Mindful eating is something I taught Nicole by example rather than training. It's a choice that each person needs to make for her or himself.

Nicole tells me she remembers our mealtimes as comforting. Long after she forgot some expensive toy I bought her, she remembered the atmosphere at the table where she learned how to relate with others, to relax and enjoy eating, to enjoy living.

All of us, mothers included, deserve to be nurtured when we're alone. I have a friend in her eighties who lives alone. She sets a place for herself at dinner each night. She makes her dinner, lights the candles, sits down, and enjoys her meal with dignity. It took me a while before I felt worthy of preparing a meal for myself after Nicole left for college. I am learning to sit down at a beautiful table, by myself, light the candles, and eat slowly while silently enjoying the moment. Whatever the situation—single, single with one child or children, or away from family—I deserve to drink fully from life's cup. Nurturance is for everybody, not just for people in a conventional family unit.

Just as there is a time for feasting, there is also a time for fasting, for health reasons or for developing insight, to clean out the body and the consciousness. The physical value of fasting is that—when it's done wisely—it cleans toxins out of the body. The

symbolic value is that fasting empties out the past. It brings me
into the present moment and can be a valuable ritual to remind
me to stay simple. I can then share that simplicity with Nicole by
providing her with a mother who is clear and present. Fasting can
be illuminating like the burning of the old leaves in autumn. It's
no coincidence that most religions have rituals that involve fasting. Saint Clement wrote: "Fasting is better than prayer."

I spend time preparing a beautiful meal and a beautiful table.
Within a short period of time the meal is gone and the table is
covered with dirty dishes and soiled napkins. We humans crave
permanency. If we're going to create art we want it to be appreciated for time immemorial. A painting will last longer than a feast,
but the creator of the painting and the creator of the feast will
both leave this planet, and all they'll leave behind is the lives
they've touched. Everything is impermanent. My teacher, Anagarika, impressed this upon me when I was struggling with the
option of whether to have a baby or to pursue a career in art. She
said, "What's one more painting in a museum. The museums are
full of paintings." It brings to mind the elaborate Tibetan sand
paintings that the monks spend days creating and then blow away
in a single afternoon.

I still paint and write and play music, but the art I leave behind is only the footprints of my spiritual journey. Ultimately,
spiritually, it doesn't matter which I do, paint a painting with
awareness or cook a meal with awareness. There's nothing tangible to show for the art of nurturance in the end except the work of
cleaning up. Even though the meal is eaten and there are dishes to
be cleaned afterward, the state of mind I'm in at the time, the vi-
bration I put out into the atmosphere can be just as powerful as a
work of art in effecting changes in others and in myself.

Cooking and eating mindfully is a happy way to live. Nicole
and I strengthen our bond each time we share a meal. Eating a

meal can be joyful; sitting down to a meal with friends and family can be a celebration. Taking care of each other and ourselves in these ways is deeply nourishing. My home is my temple, and I prepare the temple for the sacred ceremony of breaking bread. The spiritual practice around food begins as soon as I feel the intent to nurture. Through both cooking and eating we can remember what is real, celebrating our presence on this planet in a human form.

CLEANING

Centering

The time of business does not with me differ from the time of prayer, and in the noise and clatter of my kitchen, while several persons are at the same time calling for different things, I possess God in as great a tranquility as if I were on my knees at the blessed sacrament.

BROTHER LAWRENCE

It is a dewy Saturday morning and I've nowhere to be and nothing to do. Looking out through the sliding glass doors I see the spring mist hovering over the green hills, the thorny roses in their wooden-box homes, and a begging-to-be-tended garden. Nicole and I finish our cereal, get dressed in our old blue jeans and T-shirts, and make our way out of the house and into the garden.

Nicole has her own garden patch, which we call the children's garden. There she grows carrots, beets, and a host of sunflowers. As she snoops around the garden looking for interesting bugs, I settle into some overdue weeding. I begin tentatively to pull up only the largest and fiercest weeds as I walk around the garden plot. The morning sun feels soft and warm on my back, and the air around my body is alive with expectation. The fragrant earth lures me to the ground, where I find myself knuckle-deep in rich brown soil. Mercilessly I pull even the tiniest and most defenseless of the weeds.

Weeding and cleaning hold a strange and wonderful appeal for me. I remember that when I was in college I would get an urge to clean and have no place to express it. I used to hitch a ride with another student to visit my friend in Boston who had a *real home*. While she was otherwise occupied I would clean her apartment, not blatantly, not obviously, but inch by inch in an unobtrusive manner.

I usually kept my wanton enjoyment of cleaning a well-guarded secret. When I told my husband one day—I couldn't stand it any longer, I had to confess—that I found lining cupboards extremely satisfying, he just smiled, looked at me quizzically, and replied, "Go for it."

I have since confessed this forbidden pleasure of mine to other friends and was relieved to find that I was not alone. Some of my friends confided in me (I'll omit their names in case they are not yet out of this particular closet) that they got pleasure from doing their laundry, folding little sleepers, putting fresh clean sheets on beds, folding and stacking, hanging and ironing, sweeping, dusting, oiling, wiping counters, and various other perversions.

I sometimes think there is a real conspiracy in our culture against the enjoyment of housework or of any menial work for that matter. Somewhere the assumption has been made that menial work is an unworthy occupation of our time and must be finished as quickly as possible so that *real* life can resume. The tragedy of this assumption is that it makes a large portion of our lives seem meaningless. We feel unhappy when we are working, as if we are wasting our lives on inconsequential details.

I decided to explore the rewards of cleaning and organizing by talking with friends and looking within myself for some insight. I began with the assumption that those who found cleaning a pleasure were finding that pleasure in a desirable end result—a clean and comfortable home. Certainly clean sheets and well-organized cupboards are comforting, but after a closer examination of that assumption, I realized that there are people who live in spotless homes and yet feel resentful and unhappy. Their homes are like mausoleums with rooms too perfect to be enjoyed or lived in. After looking more deeply I saw that at the heart of a satisfying relationship with cleaning is not the outcome but the process. The process of mindful cleaning and organizing can be healing. It can be an opportunity to become centered and more attentive to the moment, more simple. After a challenging week, and while the children are playing or the baby is sleeping, cleaning affords an opportunity to create a refuge from the messiness of everyday living.

Marion Mountain, in *Zen Environments,* talks about her experience of everyday tasks in her Zen Buddhist practice. She writes: "For a long time I looked upon my work as a means to an end. It was only after I began to look upon the work itself as an end that the work began to unfold its unlimited possibilities. In order to realize our work fully we must do it for the sake of itself." And Sue Bender, in her book *Plain and Simple,* writes: "The Amish find meaning in work itself. Work is never viewed as a stepping stone to personal success or advancement but as a challenge to do whatever you are doing to the best of your ability." The product of a clean house is a secondary gain; the most important thing is awareness.

When I feel unhappy, angry, or confused, cleaning is something that I can do to bring me back to the present moment and help me let go of unpleasant mind states. One dusty summer day I was home with a teething baby. The air was thick and still, and the house was like an oven. I had a headache, all my muscles were tight and sore, and I felt lonely and terribly irritable. The baby was crying and needed my constant attention. I couldn't handle it anymore, so finally I stuck the baby in her crib. She continued to scream as I went into the kitchen to face a sink full of dirty dishes. I broke down and cried bitter tears. Pulling myself together, staring into the sink, I thought, "Those dishes need to be done. There's no conceivable way for me to do what I want to do, which is go off by myself and curl up into a ball, so I'll just have to center myself right where I am." I put my baby in the baby backpack and began washing each dish, one at a time, with awareness. I picked up the first plate, filled my green sponge with dish soap, turned on the hot water, mixed it with some cool water—ah, that felt so good—till it was just the right temperature. Picking up one dish, I felt its cool smoothness, its bumpy texture. Wiping off the spaghetti clinging to the surface, I rubbed my green sponge against it until it had no traces of last night's dinner, then placed it upright on the drainboard. I picked up the next dish, and the next, and the next. By the time the dishes were done I was in a powerful state of calm. My restlessness and fear had lifted, and in their place came a lightness, a clarity, and an openheartedness.

Nothing in my circumstances had changed. The baby still clung to me, although her crying had stopped and she seemed more relaxed. The air was heavy and hot, and my body still ached, only now I had let go of my desire to have things be a certain way. Now I felt content rather than miserable in the same situation. The change was sudden, like the flip of a coin.

There is something so perfectly simple about washing each dish, one by one. Each dish offers a new opportunity to practice awareness. The distinct beginning and end of the task makes it a perfect place to become mindful, since the task is not too huge to engage in with total attention. After one dish is cleaned with more or less awareness, then there is the next dish, and thus the next opportunity to practice awareness.

Homemakers understand the healing nature of cleaning and beautifying. A woman buys a flower to set on her table and then sees that she needs to oil the table so that it will reflect the beauty of the flower. Then the other pieces of furniture in the room look drab and dusty beside the shiny table. She oils the other pieces of furniture in the room to complement the beauty of the table, moving from one task to the next until the entire house has been transformed. Like unraveling a piece of cloth, cleaning one thing leads naturally to another until our home is returned to its original, natural simplicity and order.

I have a friend who finds great joy in doing her laundry. She takes the wet laundry out into the morning sun and hangs it on the line. Her toddler runs in and out of the fresh sweet sheets. What kind of memories are being created for this boy who shares the sun and clean sheets with a mother contented to be where she is? She folds the little sleepers that her children will be dreaming in and the big man-sized flannel shirts her husband will wear on Saturday when he works in the backyard. It is so sensual, so intimate to fold the laundry of the people we love. D. H. Lawrence writes: "We are transmitters . . . kindling the life-quality where it was not, even if it's only in the whiteness of a washed pocket-handkerchief."

There is nothing new about cleaning as a meditative process. The Carmelite order of Catholic monks use everyday tasks as a prayer, and in Zen Buddhist monasteries it is the senior monk who is given the job of garbage collecting and the eldest most enlightened monks who are given the opportunity to clean the toilets. Women throughout the world, for ages, have used cleaning as a centering process, although they may not have called it that.

The more awareness I bring to the task, the greater the opportunity for enlightenment. I have experienced some of my most transcendent moments while washing dishes at the sink during difficult times. When I am cleaning I am working things out, unloading the unnecessary baggage, thoughts, and feelings that I continually acquire throughout the day. I am working out greed, anger, and confusion, working them out of my consciousness to make room for the present moment. At the end of a cleaning meditation, the house is in order and my mind is at peace. The house becomes infused with a sense of mindfulness that is felt by my child and all who enter. The home becomes a temple filled with awareness and inspiration for others to find the same simplicity and clarity within themselves.

But even the grandest of human endeavors can turn sour when attachment sets in. Sometimes I find myself holding on to my homemaking too tightly, forgetting that homemaking is just a path and not who I am. When I create my identity from my homemaking activities, I lose the flexibility that is required to let my family members clean in their own way. I end up carrying the burden alone.

Maybe family members don't clean the same way I do, but sharing the tasks makes the home more theirs. It also allows them to discover some of the pleasures of cleaning. Sometimes I need to just take a deep breath and say, "Honey, I need your help folding these towels," and be ready to place little balls of terry cloth into the linen closet. Inviting family members to clean, letting them discover the personal value in the process of cleaning, is one of my many responsibilities as a teacher and keeper of the hearth.

One day, while Nicole was in school, I stayed home and cleaned the house from stem to stern. The house was beautiful when I was done, not an unessential element anywhere. Nicole came home from school and immediately began to organize a corner of the living room and make it into her store. She neatly put little things up on the walls, organized her crayons, and put her papers in neat piles. The way she responded to my love of organizing and cleaning disrupted my *House Beautiful,* but what a delight to see the joy of organizing transmitted to Nicole without a word. Example is always the best teacher. What a shame it would be if the perfection of my house became more important than my daughter's growth and development.

Besides the meditation of everyday chores, there is the larger order of the home. Where things are placed and the amount of stuff I possess sets up the framework in which the meditation of maintenance occurs. Sri Ramakrishna once said to his wife, Sri Sarata Devi, also known as Holy Mother, "In arranging objects of domestic use one must think out beforehand where particular articles are to be kept. What was frequently required must be kept near at hand and other things at a distance. When an article was temporarily removed from its place it should be put back in exactly the same place so that one might not fail to find it even in the dark."

Orderliness creates a context for mindfulness. When I open a cupboard and find neatly folded sheets, pillow cases, towels, and blankets, I am reminded of an orderly mind state. The inside of the cupboard becomes my teacher by reminding me to remain simple.

Order is essential to energy efficiency. When things are placed where I can easily find them, energy that I would have spent looking for them is conserved. There is more time to create and more lightness of heart to bring to the creative process.

While mothering I learned to carefully choose the objects I brought into our home. The more objects I have, the more things I am responsible for and have to be master of. As the quantity of material items increases, the burden gets heavier and heavier until housework becomes overwhelming. I am not a housewife, that is, I am not married to my house. My home is there to serve me as long as I remain its master. A simpler home is a more manageable servant. The products of living simply are mental lightness, more time for loving, and less time spent on unnecessary tasks.

Periodically I go through the cupboards and sort out items that are no longer useful to me. It's amazing how much clutter accumulates during moments of unconsciousness. Clutter is a way of avoiding the true emptiness of the heart. Uncluttering our lives leaves us free to enjoy the innate joy of the heart.

Material objects are just tools. When I take care of my tools, I save money on repairs and duplication of lost or misplaced objects. In this throwaway culture, we need to learn to take care of our tools and each other. When I maintain my tools with respect I am respecting the natural resources of the planet. I am remaining conscious of my transitory life on a planet that will be passed on to future generations. Nicole learns good stewardship from these everyday demonstrations.

Housework has been described as a prayer by some and as a meditation by others. It is granted the deepest respect by those transcendent beings who teach us about love and harmony. It is a practice, and like all practices there are times I feel like doing it and times I don't feel like doing it. Just as a musician who practices her scales everyday knows, the times of greatest resistance can be the times when we experience the most profound breakthroughs. Liking, disliking, wanting, not wanting—we can watch all these mind states without judgment. It's so liberating to discover that I don't need to be attached to these thoughts because in one moment wanting turns to not wanting and not liking turns to liking. Impermanence and change are part of the human condition, and they affect cleaning just as they affect all other endeavors large and small.

However I begin the process of cleaning, with enthusiasm or with disdain, I try to stay mindful of the process. I wash the floor and am aware of its golden color, its smooth texture, and the spaces of built-up dirt. My mind wanders off to a song I'm working on. I notice the wandering and bring my attention back to the floor. Washing, washing, washing. Nicole is calling me. Stopping, listening, speaking, returning. Washing, washing, washing. Oh, I forgot to call Nancy about the meeting. Thinking, planning.

We walk the middle path neither by hanging on to the pleasant thoughts and feelings nor by getting sucked down into the mire of the lows. The feelings and thoughts just come and go. To hang on to any one of them is as impossible as hanging on to September 20, 1987, 8:45 A.M., on a dewy Sonoma morning in the garden, bending, touching the weed, plucking, lifting, feeling glad, breathing in, out, in, out.

JOYFUL SERVICE

Selfless Service

Service which is rendered without joy helps neither the servant nor the served. But all other pleasures pale into nothingness before service which is rendered in a spirit of joy.

MAHATMA GANDHI

When Nicole's father and I separated I needed to find work outside the home. Like thousands of other women I became what was then called a "displaced housewife and single mom." Having been content to be at home raising my little one, I was now being forced out of my home and into the world. Even so I was committed to being home for Nicole as much as possible. It was clear to me that starting a career would take great quantities of time and energy, so I chose to take a job that would provide immediate money and would allow me to spend more time with Nicole. Since I'd felt drawn to nursing homes since I can remember, I became a nurse's aide at a local extended-care facility. After a few months of grueling work at minimum wage as a nurse's aide I was offered a job singing in nursing homes through the local junior college. Being offered this job was one of those miraculous demonstrations of how, when we follow our hearts, doors appear where we previously saw none.

There could not have been a better job for me. It was an opportunity to be with the elders and to sing the American popular standards I love so much that I would sing them for free. Many elders are beyond the need to conform or to impress others. So much has been taken from them, so much chiseled away, that they are forced to be more authentic. Humans tend to cling to pain and relive its old familiar drama, holding on to it like comfortable old shoes that we hate but can't bear to let go of. We cling to memories of how our mothers dealt with situations, to ideas about ourselves as being "professional," "well brought up," "rebels," "artists," "mothers," "Irish," "black sheep," as if these old labels really define who we are, as if our identities are the whole purpose and meaning of our existence. This is why I love to be in nursing homes.

It was a hard time in my life. I was raising a child by myself, was occasionally in unhappy romantic relationships, and was beginning to have health challenges. Yet, as painful as life felt to me, my difficulties paled before the hardships of the elders I was serving. I had lost my marriage and my sense of purpose, but they had lost so much more. They had lost their homes, their friends, their mobility, and their freedom in the world. They were saying good-bye to everything as they watched their time on this planet draw to a close.

Before singing in nursing homes I reveled in the catharsis I felt while singing sad, haunting ballads like "Here's the Rainy Day" and "Cry Me a River." In the nursing homes I might just as well have put arsenic in their water as sing those sad songs. They didn't need to get in touch with their sorrow; they were swimming in it. They needed to be lifted up to see a brighter world, if only for one hour. If I had ignored what they needed and just sang what I felt like singing, I would have been engaging in miserly giving. My job was to serve them, not to be self-serving, and when I strayed from an upbeat message, I immediately lost my audience. The elders were not subtle about letting me know when I was off course. They would ask to be wheeled out of the room or start shouting at relatives on the other side of this dimension. I did not have to read between their lines. Their responses could not have been clearer had they been well-aimed tomatoes. By lifting their spirits during this difficult juncture in my life, I lifted myself up as well. I would leave the nursing homes feeling better than when I went in. I received much support and appreciation from the elders, and as time went on we became family.

When I was able to see my own sorrow in the context of a broader perspective it diminished in importance. When my identification with my own sorrow lost some of its power, energy that went into maintaining that ego identification naturally flowed into serving others joyfully. This life of ours is a little flash of lightning in the vast sky, and there is nothing more important than using the energy of that flash to charge the air around us with love.

I was serving the elders at work and serving Nicole at home. I had always thought of service as going off to India to work with Mother Teresa or as joining the Peace Corps. It didn't even occur to me that raising a child would be an act of spiritual service. I was to discover that mothering is the model for selfless service.

Women come to service naturally. Our wombs are designed to give birth; our breasts are designed to give milk. We are biologically constructed to nurture in order to perpetuate the species. Service is a core aspect of feminine psychology and spirituality. In our materialistic culture this natural generosity and delight in giving has been abused and misunderstood. The desire to serve has often been misinterpreted as a weakness by women and men alike. Since it is natural for women to serve without looking for reward, they have often been unappreciated, undervalued, and underpaid.

A lack of respect for the woman who is happy to serve her family and community is epidemic in our culture. The homemaker is busy keeping the home warm and taking care of children all day yet given precious little recognition, materially or otherwise, for her service. A seventy-year-old great-grandmother who found herself spending her retirement years in poverty said, "There is no recognition for all the hard work women do, and it really hits home when you retire and see how low your compensation is."

Out of anger and hurt, many women I know have cut themselves off from their natural feminine generosity. Some women have come to view service as demeaning. One friend told me she didn't want to waste her life "giving it away." Some women I have talked to feel that material power is more important than their inner spiritual power, and as a result they have lost a precious part of their spiritual feminine birthright.

When I worked as a nurse's aide I was paid minimum wage and treated like I was a second-class citizen. I learned from this experience how many valuable mothers, teachers, nurses, social workers, and day-care providers are undervalued and underpaid in our culture. Yet, what is more important than nurturing the next generation or the elders who nurtured us? We all get sick, we all die, and some of us become elderly. It is the essence of each one of us, not our exterior or material value, that is so precious. If money is the designator of worth in our culture, and we pay minimum wages to the person who tends our children and our elderly while richly compensating the person who produces deodorant commercials, what message are we giving our children?

There are so many angels among us who wish to serve from the heart but can't afford to do so. I was in the supermarket one day talking with the woman who was checking out my groceries. She had been in nurse's aide training with me, and I asked her if she was doing any nursing now. She said that she had worked as a nurse's aide for about nine months after our training and had treated all her patients as if they were her own grandparents. She got scolded by the management for spending too much time with each patient. She told her boss that she couldn't care for patients properly in the time allotted to her, got into a big fight with the administration, and left nursing to become a checkout person at the grocery store. She went further than most aides would go by letting the administration know how she felt. Most just suffer the abuse, burn out, and leave. Intelligent, cost-effective management would support those who provide hands-on care by respecting them and paying them well.

Serving the elders and Nicole was a joyful experience for me. I learned what it meant to transcend my ego. The veil of illusion, the illusion that I am separate, was temporarily lifted whenever I engaged in joyful service. I experienced a release of my ego's powerful hold on me as I merged with the beloved I was serving. Transcending the small self and merging with whomever we serve is at the core of joyful service. It is then that service becomes a mystical experience and we spend our days and nights deeply in love.

I experience this merging when I'm *in love* and suddenly see the color of the stars and hear the breeze through the eucalyptus trees as if for the first time. Everything is new and bright and magical. I experience this freedom from the ego when I create or hear beautiful music or when the solution to a problem becomes clear. There are certain peak experiences, a feeling of being at one with my environment, my loved ones, my self, and the whole universe. I experience this blissful merging more and more often in my life as I surrender more fully to joyful service.

I learned that the surrender of ego must precede selfless service. When I went into service expecting some personal gain, I was invariably disappointed. Although serving others does entail personal gain, that gain is seldom realized when we've made it our intent. Only when the intent is the happiness, comfort, and joy of the person being served do we reap the abundant harvest of selfless service.

When I mentally fly up above my life and look down on it, I see how short it is, how many others exist who are at the center of their own dramas, how insignificant my dramas are in the grand scheme of things. In a hundred years no one is going to care if my child played hooky from school, yet these things are extremely important to me at the time. Of course we need to meet the challenges of life, but the amount of suffering we experience as we deal with these challenges is proportional to how identified we are with the issue at hand. We have choices here.

As the burden of ego identification is lifted, our natural generosity emerges. When that happens I cease to care if the world around me says I am wasting my time raising my child or caring for a person in need. I am listening to what my heart wants me to do. When my eyes are opened and cleansed of the debris of ego, I see the pain around me clearly. I see the children coming home from school to empty houses. I see the elderly aching to be touched and heard. I see people homeless and dying of malnutrition. I see lonely people starving for love. My heart opens with compassion. I know what happiness feels and smells like and want to share it with others.

Joyful service is not an easy path to follow, but it is richly rewarding. I love to serve so much that I sometimes end up taking care of people at my own expense. Some years ago I discovered that I was collecting *friends* who needed healing and took it upon myself to be their healer. It was a thankless task and instead of being selfless service, it turned out to more closely resemble codependance. It turned out to be my own need I was trying to fill. I had a friend who kept going out on alcoholic binges. After ago-nizing over how to save him I realized that even if I turned my life upside down to accommodate his cure it would not help. For him to heal he needed to choose healing. Meanwhile I stood helpless, waiting for him to choose life. It was a difficult but valuable lesson. I learned that selfless service does not mean neglecting oneself to serve others. If I neglect nurturing and taking care of myself I deplete my resources and have nothing left to give. I do not serve others wisely this way and can even inhibit their growth by rushing in to *save* them before they learn the lessons that life is bringing them.

The giving of joyful service is like a well-nourished rosebush offering two roses where one is cut. The joyful server comes from a place of abundance and overflow; that's the only way selflessness can be genuine. If the server is needy she is bound to become burnt out by serving, and all her good intentions will get washed away by the current. Before giving selflessly, a person must have a healthy happy self to release.

There are many spiritual and psychological benefits I have gained in the occupation of joyful service. When I let go of my own troubles to help another person I find moments of relief from the tape of my own problems. Serving in this way is not the same as running away from problems or losing myself in another. Rather, it serves the same purpose as meditation. When my attention is fixed on a positive course, loving another, that focus can change the course of my mind. By taking a break from my negative thinking I can shift the course of my thoughts from destructive to productive.

When I am serving joyfully I develop generosity and a sense of abundance, which I can then pass on to Nicole. By loving others I open myself to receiving that same love in return. When I selflessly take care of Nicole she learns by example how to provide loving care for others. She thus grows up and extends care to others, thereby building a rich, loving network. These are just some of the fruits of joyful service that motherhood brought me.

Joyful service opens the door to an awareness of the infinite abundance that has always been there waiting to be tapped. The more I give from a joyful state of mind, the more I have to give. It's like the fairy tale about the poor fisherman who gave shelter to an angel disguised as a beggar and received a magic coin that increased in amount every time he spent it. By giving joyfully I've discovered that there is more than enough to go around and have become more and more openhanded in my giving. I've learned to live with a sense of abundance rather than scarcity. Generosity increases with use. This is true magic! Yet this magic only works when I give with a joyful heart. My mind can't be tricked. It knows my true intentions.

Joyful service connects us with those around us. When we feel alienated, separate from other people, from life, from ourselves, we are prone to addictions, depression, and illness. I have a friend who was recently divorced. One Christmas her children were with their father, her relatives were way back East, and she didn't have the money for an airplane ticket to visit them. After spending some time with her sadness she decided to go to a homeless shelter and work in the cafeteria on Christmas Day. Later that week she called me up, all bubbly and excited. She told me, "I got into making the tables beautiful for the people. I wiped up the dust, set the tables, put out some flowers that were growing outside the building. I got so caught up in what I was doing that I didn't notice that this man was watching me. He said, 'This isn't the royal palace, you know!' I was so absorbed in making the place beautiful that until he spoke I was unaware of how my consciousness had been altered. I just laughed and smiled. I felt like I was meditating, not just cleaning up at a soup kitchen. It was a wonderful Christmas. I sat down with him and the others and felt like a part of a big grateful family." I hear this kind of story over and over from people who engage in joyful service. They are surprised at the depth of happiness they experience and how serving others takes them out of their own suffering.

When I am able to get myself out of the way and unobtrusively enter another person's reality I experience the bliss of timelessness and union. We can experience this kind of bliss in a mansion or in a tenement. Outer conditions do not create or affect this state of bliss. The depth of the happiness and peace of mind that comes from selfless service is not like the transitory happiness of receiving material goods, which can foster a hunger for more. Rather, the joy of selfless service is a genuinely unshakable, timeless happiness.

There is no score card in joyful service, no quid pro quo. We mothers give service without any thought of gain. We can feel joy as we nurture our loved ones, cooking dinner night after night or putting shells by our children's bed so that they may see nature's beauty all around them.

There is a simplicity and a loving attention to detail when service is rendered joyfully. Recipients of heartfelt service feel more comfortable receiving because they do not feel guilty, as if they owe the server something in return for the service. The mother who serves joyfully is mentally and emotionally present with her children, not thinking about work or other things that have to be done, not resenting the time spent walking slowly with a curious toddler. The details of our days become beautiful moments of presence. The child can relax and be nourished, not only by the care he is receiving but also by this living example of happiness in the moment.

When rendering joyful service I am providing my family with an example of what being a happy person looks like, which is perhaps the greatest gift of all. Mother Teresa said, "A smile must always be on our lips for any child to whom we offer help, for any to whom we give companionship or medicine. It would be very wrong to offer only our cures; we must offer to all our heart." This attitude is valuable at all times but particularly when we are caring for our children, our elders, and those who are in pain. They are very sensitive to our intent. Sue Bender writes that for the Amish woman "[a]ll her duties were an expression of her love for her family and for God. The extra hours she spent quilting tiny stitches expressed her love for the person who would receive the quilt."

I have a friend who brings a fresh glass of water to her husband's bedside table each night. When he goes for his water he is drinking her love. I have another friend who sits down with her child at the piano as she practices. She puts her full attention on the child for a half hour each day. There are a million ways we serve our friends and loved ones everyday: making meals, reading to them, driving them to appointments, seeing that they do their homework, running errands, paying the bills. There is no glory in the well-changed diaper, only the discovery of simple moments of surrender, with sweet eyes looking up lovingly.

The opposite of joyful service is poisonous martyrdom. It is often through this process of disrespect for those who serve that mothers become martyrs. Martyrdom is *self-ful* service. There is a desire for some gain for the service rendered even as the martyr is expecting no reward to be forthcoming. In place of the reward comes bitterness and resentment toward those who are being served. Martyrs do not meet their own needs directly but instead try to meet them covertly through the guilt they provoke in others.

As mothers we are called upon to serve not just from nine to five but whenever our children need us. Oftentimes we are called upon to serve when we don't feel like serving. We might be sick, and our baby might also be sick. Regardless of our own condition, we need to take care of our sick baby. Mothers find themselves in this situation all the time. There is a meeting we want to go to, but something suddenly happens to one of our children and we must put our own plans aside.

Through practice we train ourselves to serve joyfully even when we don't initially feel generous and openhearted. It is a practice, like learning to sing by repeating scales over and over until the line becomes fluid. It doesn't always spring forth fully developed. Sometimes there is the need to bring consciousness to a situation in order to change an old habit. Rabbi Nachman of Bratslau observed: "Always be joyful, no matter what you are. With happiness you can give a person life. Every day we must de- liberately induce in ourselves a buoyant, exuberant attitude toward life. In this manner, we gradually become receptive to the sub- tle mysteries around us. And if no inspired moments come, we should act as though we have them anyway. If you have no enthu- siasm, put up a front. Act enthusiastic and the feeling will be- come genuine."

Practicing happiness is not phoniness or putting on a plastic smile. Anger and sadness are important emotions, valuable sig- nals that something is wrong or that there is a need for change. But we are the artists of our lives, and our emotions are only the colors that we work with. The effort to transcend a negative state of mind must come from our hearts through our own heart's de- sire for happiness.

Dogen Zenju said, "Observe how even animals and insects nurture their young, enduring hardships in the process. The par- ents stand to gain nothing by their actions even after their off-spring have reached maturity. Yet, though they are only small creatures, they have deep compassion for their young. This is also the case with regard to various Buddhas' compassion for all sentient beings." What better place to develop compassion for all sentient beings than in the home, where we learn how to serve our loved ones without thought of reward while our hearts fill with joy.

EXTENDED FAMILY

Karmic Relationships

Until we heal original relationships, we'll never truly be in fresh relationships with others.

JOHN BRADSHAW, author and family counselor

My dad had driven the twenty minutes from his home in Oakmont to meet me for dinner in Sonoma. We met at a coffee shop in a shopping center that had a supermarket, a bagel shop, and a Rite Aid drugstore. We ate our sandwiches and caught up on news about Nicole, the house, Dad's lady friend, sharing warm feelings. When we finished eating we left arm in arm and walked around the shopping center on a mission to find a single razor blade for his shaver. We ended up in the Rite Aid and walked down each isle commenting on the products. "This is an interesting Thermos. I wonder how they figured out how to make one of these things!" We just strolled down the aisles as if we were sightseeing along Fifth Avenue and with as much pleasure as if we were in Wonderland. When we turned the corner on the gardening aisle there in front of us was a stone that had the words "Heaven on Earth" written on it. We just stood in front of that stone and gazed at it. Yes, this was heaven on earth.

My father always had a way of making magic out of small things. He would bring home some sample fabric pamphlets from a sewing store and deliver them to me in piles and piles. I was overjoyed by the colors and textures and by the abundance of it all. He taught me how to swim, ride a bike, water-ski, horseback-ride, and drive a car. His office was in back of our home, so he was always around, and even when he was distracted by work I felt his presence. It took me the longest time to figure out what he did for a living. When I was in elementary school I made up stories about his occupation. I filled the puzzling gap of reality with anything I fancied. He was a zookeeper, a carnival operator, and some sort of Hawaiian warrior king. Whatever he was, or wasn't, he was there. I know what it's like to feel perfectly cozy and safe in my father's arms.

Friends who see me with my father now tell me how lucky I am to have such a great relationship with him. I assure them that it was not always that way. There have been times I hated him, times when I went toe to toe with him on core issues. There were times when months and months would go by without us speaking to each other or when we sent caustic letters back and forth. No, this has not been an easy relationship but a hard-won, at times truly raw, and usually honest one. There were times I just wanted him to disappear, but he was my father forever and always, and primary family members do not ever disappear; even after death we carry them with us.

There are those who say we choose our parents and those who say it's the luck of the draw. I can't say for certain which is true, but I do know that our families remain a primary influence on us, affecting everything in our lives, including our spiritual work. We are dealt a certain hand of cards when we are born. Whether or not we had choice in the dealing of those cards, we do have a choice regarding how we play them. How we choose to deal with our primary family, our karmic relations, greatly affects our parenting. It serves us as mothers and as spiritual aspirants to come to terms with the strengths and weaknesses of the family into which we were born.

My karmic family had its fair share of dysfunction. There was tension, anger, unmet expectations, blowups, and tight stomachs. As a child I withdrew into my imagination as my older brother threatened to blow up the elementary school and my younger brother put a lot of energy into being good and keeping out of the way. My father was tense and frustrated and angry a lot of the time, and my mother was running around outside of her body trying to make everything nice. Yet, we had three saving graces: first, my parents' deep love of family; second, an inner urging to uncover what was going wrong; and third, sincere effort to heal the pain and dysfunction. My karmic family was forever working on our healing, thanks to my mother, who carried a vision of a better way and was committed to the realization of that vision. My mother taught each of us the value of communication and introspection. I am grateful for these gifts, which have helped me find happiness and a path to that happiness that I can share with others.

It's a wonderful thing when your family members look out for one another, when you have a mother or sister or brother or father or grandparent nearby to help with the children, to share holidays with, to sit down for a cup of tea with, to be there in times of need. This closeness is one of life's greatest blessings. A supportive extended family gives life substance during the good times and a cushion during the hard times. It is the karmic net that is there to catch us when we make the inevitable learning mistakes of life, when we have an unexpected illness or financial crisis, and when all other doors seem closed to us. Many people I know are very sad because they do not have a strong karmic net. Strong family connectedness is important at all times but especially so when one is starting a family. When I was beginning my own family, what worked and what didn't work with my extended family of origin became magnified.

My karmic family, the people I grew up with, the people who were around when I was a child—aunts, uncles, parents, siblings, grandparents—are the people with whom I have the most unfinished business and to whom I am the most deeply connected. I find it to be of great value to regard my extended family with eyes that are as open, clear, and nonjudgmental as I am able to manage in the moment. Although I may feel justified in criticizing my family, being critical doesn't help me heal karmic wounds. These are the wounds placed in our path to guide us to our ultimate spiritual growth. Looking back on it, every karmic wound that I was able to heal, or even partially heal, gave my own child a stronger foundation for finding her own path. I heal by going back to the home front and observing the origin of my conditioning without blame, with an open heart. I have found this to be the single most powerful way to gain insight into myself, what I love, what I hate, and where I learned my habits.

My father grew up with a tough and ruthless father and a mother who was depressed and angry. He watched his father being unfaithful to his mother. He saw his mother use the only power she felt she had, her sexuality, in sad and inappropriate ways. His parents were cruel to one another and to their children. The battle of the sexes was bloody and vicious in my family of origin. I remember my father telling me, "If a woman is raped she probably brought it on herself." For ages men of many cultures have been blaming women for the sexual feelings they have toward women. Anger and distrust between men and women is one of my greatest family shadows. Women in my father's family were delegated to being nurturers and sexual objects. I grew up in this shadow, which informed every aspect of my life. To be assertive, to be sexual, and to be independent threatened to topple this flawed structure and made the realization of my womanhood difficult and threatening. I know that I share this experience with many women the world over.

At this point in history it is easy for women to spend a large portion of their lives reacting to the false thought form of women being inferior to men. After all, it's been operative for thousands of years. Many of us are run by this pattern, which shows up in our relationships with men and in a hesitancy to fully embrace our own power. What a gift it is to be able to walk into our parents' home with eyes wide open and see the pattern laid out before us. In my own life it was not pleasant to see my beloved father's hostile behavior toward my own gender. It was painful to watch my mother struggle between her dependence on my father and her need to be a fully realized human being. Women today have many more options than previous generations had for breaking these ancient, recurring patterns. I must confess that despite these options I have often thought of myself as a victim. I have embraced the limiting belief that all men are bad. I have even believed that women are weak and men are strong. I have also believed that men are weak and women strong. I thought that my parents were twisted and stayed away from them. Now I see that the karmic patterns of our families have been passed down to us to be healed, passed down to our mothers from their mothers and on back till . . . when? Do we want to perpetuate the karmic wounds or heal them? And if we choose to heal the wounds, what do we do? Since the first step in healing anything is to clearly identify the problem, that is what I finally chose to do after much reacting and being at the affect of the pattern.

I brought the information I gleaned from my family visits back home with me and watched how the wounds and patterns had affected my relationship with Nicole, with men, with my own power, with my career. I saw, as so many other women have, that I had given up my power to feel loved. In my relationship with Nicole it took the form of having difficulty sticking to limits. With men it took the form of choosing men who were abusive. With my career it took the form of having low expectations of my earning power. And in my spiritual work it took the form of the question "How could little lowly me be someone with all the power and joy there is?" This pattern seeped into every aspect of my life. Returning to my family of origin gave me a great opportunity to see where the habits of powerlessness came from and how they operated so that I could heal them on a deep level. Today we see a bigger picture: that we are all healing this planet, person by person, and family by family. Everything I heal in my family pattern in relation to the mutual distrust of men and women is being healed not only for myself but for my entire family tree and for men and women everywhere.

Family is where the profound and ancient work is. The work of accepting my karmic family as it is has been an essential step toward accepting myself as I am, of coming to terms with the things I dislike most about myself, of seeing my own dark side and being able to forgive myself and my family. I am developing not blind acceptance of things as they are but a real clarity about what's going on and an acceptance of the fact that we are, after all, only human. It would be folly for me to think that I retain only the positive conditioning of my ancestors. The positive conditioning is wonderful. I can enjoy and appreciate it. But the negative conditioning spurs me on to find deeper happiness and relaxation within myself, and so it is a rich place to visit on my quest toward greater happiness and spiritual insight. Going into those tight, painful places and unlatching the patterns, one by one, is an important aspect of the enlightenment process and an invaluable contribution to conscious mothering.

Some spiritual aspirants go off and practice in exotic locations far from their families and other distractions. I have met many meditators who would like to just meditate their family conditioning away without turning and facing that conditioning with an open, vulnerable heart. Part of the work along the path to enlightenment is cleaning out the corners of our karmic heritage. There is a Buddhist story about a monk who spent twenty-five years up in a mountain cave meditating. A yogi came to visit this meditator and asked him, "What are you practicing?" The meditator replied, "I am practicing the perfection of patience." The yogi replied, "Wonderful!" and proceeded to throw things around the cave, eat the man's food, and make a general nuisance of himself. The meditator was getting upset, and the yogi cranked up the volume by tearing up his book and messing up his shrine. Finally, the meditator got up and started screaming at the yogi, and the yogi said, "Ah, and now where is your perfection of patience?" What good is my peace of mind if it cannot be brought into the everyday world? When I climb back down from that protective mountain I am once again faced with the same old baggage I left at the foothills. My baggage is waiting there for me like the patient teacher it truly is.

As a spiritual aspirant and as a mother it is my job to follow the guidance of my higher self under hostile and difficult conditions as well as under friendly or easy ones. I can't think of anything more difficult than going back to my family of origin and practicing nonjudgmental awareness and forgiveness. My family has the power to push all of my hidden buttons. It is a virtual research library into my conditioning. Peace begins in the home not just as a facade but as the very seeds that bring forth real fruit. In order to create a peaceful new family I need to make peace within myself, with my family of origin, my karmic family.

Honoring your father and your mother is part of many great spiritual practices. But honoring our parents is not the same as feeling obligated to honor them blindly. Rather, it's about a deeper inner gratitude for their having given us the gift of life. Obligation is toxic; honoring is joyful. My mother carried me for nine months in her womb. The Buddha said that to be given a human incarnation is the greatest gift one being can give another because enlightenment can only be realized in human form. This is the gift my mother gave me and the one I gave Nicole—the gift of human birth. Even if our parents deserted us, they at least gave us the opportunity to take human form. Deep gratitude for this gift can be difficult for some of us. Honoring our parents, even for the pain they caused us, the pain that gives us the opportunity to develop compassion, frees us to create more and deeper love in our lives. Even the problems, especially the problems, have become gifts since I've committed to waking up.

Being able to accept my parents' humanness is an essential key to becoming whole and accepting myself. Leo Buscaglia wrote: "Maybe the point of arriving at adulthood is facing these two people, this man and this woman, and seeing them as ordinary human beings like ourselves, with hangups, with misconceptions, with tenderness, with joy, with sorrow and with tears." As I matured emotionally I opened to accepting my parents as they were and took full responsibility for my own life.

I believe that in the practice of seeing our parents' humanness we move toward acceptance and forgiveness of our own humanity. Negative conditioning is not who we are. It will melt away when it is examined with a loving heart. By empathizing with my parents', brothers', and grandparents' pain, I see how the hurt they inflicted on me was inflicted on them at a time when they were unable to shield themselves from it. Longfellow wrote: "If we could read the secret history of our enemies, we would find in each person's life sorrow and suffering enough to disarm all hostility." There can be a certain comfort in endlessly licking our wounds, but this leaves us powerless, and locked in a pattern that we pass on to our children. Taking responsibility to end negative karmic conditioning gives us the power to remold our lives in a fresh and functional way, gifting our children with the inheritance of a deep appreciation for who they are.

Until there is forgiveness there is no healing of the ancient family wounds. Forgiveness is not about being in denial or fighting to rectify old wounds. That only gives the shadow power to rear its ugly head while I sit peacefully on my meditation pillow. I used to confuse taking responsibility with accepting blame. Forgiveness is not about condoning another's injurious actions but about taking the power back from them as we come to understand the larger picture. Forgiveness is not about accepting abusive behavior or allowing it to continue. Through forgiveness, we can separate unskillful actions from the unskillful actor, and thereby reveal his or her essential nature, which is the same as mine. I learned through my love of Nicole that when she does something that hurts me I condemn her action, not her.

Whatever anyone says or does is more about them than it is about me, and I consciously make that distinction. By not taking their words or actions personally, I provide no place for the pain they are projecting to land in my consciousness. The Buddha said that if you give someone a present and they do not accept it, whose present is it? If someone gives me an insult, and I don't accept it, then it is theirs to keep.

I am grateful to have had time with my parents as I was developing insight into my true nature. When I lived back East and my parents lived in L.A. they became an abstraction to me. I romanticized our relationship and turned them into archetypes. Now they've become people to me, no longer just images. It's difficult to see my dad being harsh with Nicole and then see myself acting the same way with her. It was uncomfortable to see my mom set limits with Nicole, back off from them, and then see myself doing the same thing. But I'm grateful for the window I was given into the choices I'm making so that I can make better ones.

Since becoming a mother, I have found the connection with my ancestral roots has become even more compelling. I understand what it means to shoulder the responsibility of caring for children. I understand how difficult it is and how, no matter how hard I try, I must accept that I am imperfect. It's a humbling experience that makes forgiveness possible. The fact that my parents were the role models for how to parent is a fact of life. No matter how hard I may try to raise Nicole differently from the way I was raised, any unhealed karmic conditioning just seems to come oozing through the cracks. My shadow became obvious when I had my own child to raise, no matter how enlightened I may have thought I was. Today I am so grateful for motherhood and for what, with the help of my spiritual practice, it has taught me.

Each of us is an individual and at the same time a part of a system. Recognizing this fact is as critical in mothering as it is in the larger perspective of our spiritual practice. In a family where everything seems to be working fine, except for one child who is acting out, taking drugs, stealing, or whatever, that child is cracking open the myth of perfection in that family and providing an opportunity for that family's collective wound to be exposed to the air and to heal. Acting rather than reacting is the path away from the same old alluring scripts we are drawn to repeat unconsciously. It goes much deeper than simply asserting my needs, or calling it as I see it. As I develop spiritual maturity I learn when to say something and when to withhold the insight. Sometimes I want to say, "Dad, if you would just do this or that things would be a whole lot more peaceful around here." It's tempting to want to change others for "the better," but the fact is, it doesn't work. Everyone changes in their own time and by their own volition.

I used to be very reactive with my father. He would say something to me like "If a women wants to be loved by a man she needs to stay out of the boardroom," and I would blow up. Now when he says or does something that shakes me to my roots, I feel the shaking and take a minute to remember who I am and who he is, and I am able to stay grounded. When we are truly in our power we are not threatened by another's power. When I am in my power I can hear what is behind his words and have compassion for him and for the pain that sustains his own sense of powerlessness.

No matter how much I may understand with my head, I don't feel compassion for another until I connect with my own pain. I once went to a family practice session with Nicole at Green Gulch Farm Zen Center, where I spoke with a woman about one of my meditation teachers. She told me she didn't like this teacher because her friend had gone on retreat with him and had experienced many hindrances—anger, lust, etc. The teacher had said, "That's good; keep meditating." This attitude made the woman angry. She felt it was callous of him to speak to her friend that way. I remembered how, during retreats, just as I was about to go into a clear blissful state I would become restless, lustful, or angry. I'd find the most obscure things to be angry about. I've gone on retreats for over twenty years, and this happens each time. Retreats are great places to practice watching difficult emotions without reacting to them. There is nobody actually there to blame, so anger becomes just anger, and in this pure state we can own it as ours. Working with karmic relationships develops the inner harmony necessary for the evolving of mindfulness and calm. When I do my karmic homework before sitting down on the meditation pillow I experience less psychic noise and a clearer road, which makes it easier for me to attain deeper states of concentration. I know that my mind cannot be clear as long as I am holding onto anger and resentment.

One summer when I was on a retreat I met a man whose body was stiff with anger. He didn't smile and his face was hard. He was accustomed to practicing intense concentration meditations. This was a Vipassána retreat where we practice both mindfulness of whatever comes up and concentration on the breath. Because he was being asked to allow his thoughts to arise without interference, he was challenged to see what was there instead of allowing the tunnel vision of concentration meditation to distort the picture. He was challenged to be aware of his thoughts without directing them toward calm or anything else. During a group interview he related how unpleasant mind states had come up during his meditation. He felt that was bad, and he wanted to control his mind to have only pleasant thoughts. He asked the teacher how he could get rid of his uncomfortable thoughts and feelings. It was clear that he was trying to escape his negative karmic conditioning through meditation just as one might use a drug to escape pain.

People often come to a spiritual practice to find relief from the unpleasantness in their lives, but it doesn't work like that. We bring our karmic relations into the meditation hall with us. There's Grandma over there to the left telling us to tie our shoes, to sit up straight; there's father in front of us making sure we look like we know what we're doing; and there's mother's voice whispering that we should only think nice thoughts. If the meditator simply sits with the discomfort rather than reject uncomfortable thoughts and feelings, those uncomfortable thoughts and feelings eventually dissipate, leaving him free from suffering, truly free. He might be well served by the practice of going back to his family of origin with bare-bones awareness to watch, cry, and release his sadness so that his shadow no longer controls his meditation. If he allows himself to feel his sadness, then his heart can break open, allowing insight to come pouring through.

I used to wonder why I was born into my particular family and why I was gifted with Nicole. From remembering past lives I know that my family and I have been together many times, changing roles and learning from one another. Karmic relationships have a higher charge than most other relationships. When I first looked at Nicole's little face I realized the power and responsibility of this relationship. I believe that karmic realtionships hold the key to the lessons I need to confront in this lifetime. I now know that I am exactly where I need to be right now, that life has flow and order to it. My parents did exactly what they needed to do in order for me to have the experiences necessary for me to grow in this lifetime, and I bless them for that. Today, with Nicole growing into womanhood, I see the karmic chain that extends into the future, and I recognize anew how important it is for each of us to heal what we inherit.

Accepting my heritage is an inner experience. Working out karmic relationships doesn't involve changing anybody, not even myself. When I'm aware that I'm in a bad mood I don't need to deny it or hate myself for it; I only need to see it. As I observe my negative thinking without judgment, it begins to fade. When I turn nonjudgmental awareness onto my karmic shadow the shadow begins to dissolve. To deny my ancestral wound is playing with fire. When even one person is closed out of my heart I lose access to a part of myself. Even closing out the bum on the street who pisses on the wall or the aunt with a shrill voice who pinches my cheek! Leaving out anyone leaves an empty space in my heart. As long as I have an aversion to anyone, I have an aversion to a part of myself. We are all parts of one body.

The development of harmonious family relations is a process rather than a goal. It is the same as enlightenment. We're all enlightened to some degree, and we become more enlightened in increments. Each time we work something out on a deeper level we are that much more enlightened. If our spiritual work is to break the bonds of attachment, where better to begin than within our karmic realationships?

I would say that my family has a fairly average share of joy and pain. There have been times we have supported one another, and there have been times when our shadows have gotten in the way of giving the love we wished to give. There have been torments and twists that have gotten in the way of expressing love to one another, but love is the bottom line. My mother's least favorite thing to say was "Love is the only game in town." We continue to chisel away at our crusty surfaces in order to free the healing light of our love. We work hard, as individuals and as a family, to clear the debris in the path of loving one another. Our hard work is paying off. My mother became my beloved mentor; my father, my teacher and student; my brothers, kindred spirits; and Nicole, my best friend. We've uncovered who we really are to one another, helpmates on the path to enlightenment.

SELF-LOVE

Temple Care

It is by cultivating the thought "May I be happy" with oneself as example, that one begins to be interested in the welfare and happiness of other living beings, and to feel in some sense their happiness as if it were one's own . . . so one should first become familiar with pervading oneself as example with lovingkindness.

NANAMOLI THERA, *The Practice of Lovingkindness*
(Kandy, Ceylon: Buddhist Publication Society, 1964)

After dragging myself through half of a bedtime story I kissed Nicole good night, apologized for not being able to read any longer, and fell exhausted onto my bed. I helplessly watched the energy drain from my body as day by day my mounting exhaustion forced me to give up pieces of my life. First I gave up my social life to come home from work or school and rest. Then I gave up graduate school. Eventually I had to let go of my job singing in nursing homes, a job I loved.

I went to numerous doctors, but nobody had a clue to what the problem was. One doctor suggested I try Parents Without Partners, assuming that my problem was psychosomatic. Lying in bed, I couldn't care less whether the problem was psychosomatic or purely somatic. I could barely move or talk, and my body ached with endless flu symptoms. Descending to the border between life and death, I gave up everything except raising my daughter. There, lying in bed, unable to read or even watch TV, I surrendered to this strange force that was draining the life from my body. As I surrendered, a voice came from deep within me, reminding me that I must raise my daughter and fulfill my purpose for being here. At that moment I chose to live.

I had spent my life reluctant to join this world, wondering how I landed here on this troubled planet. After half a lifetime of living in this body halfheartedly, my whole being was crying out for me to listen to its call for exercise, rest, and, most important, for love. The Masnavi I Ma'navi wrote: "Knowest thou not the beauty of thine own face? Quit this temper that leads thee to war with thyself." I was forced by this mysterious illness to look at the war being waged within myself and to make peace with my own face, my own psyche, my human birth. I was forced by the love of my daughter to join the world wholeheartedly, to develop self-love.

Marion Mountain says, "The work of taking care of the environment also means taking care of our self. When Zen masters bid goodbye to their students and friends, they often say, 'take good care of yourself.' When you take good care of yourself you will take good care of the environment; and when you take good care of your environment, you will also take good care of yourself. You and your environment will work harmoniously to reveal your original ecological nature."

Given my strong feminine nature I delight in giving. Those of us with well-developed feminine natures are guided by our generosity and service-mindedness to take care of everybody, from our children to those starving in Ethiopia, before we take care of ourselves. We think perhaps rest will at last come when all is well in the world, but as we work to create the impossible we ourselves become more and more depleted, until we can't even take care of our own immediate environment. I gave until my body could give no more. I wore down my immune system with stress and poor care and became so out of touch with my body that I wasn't even aware of the severity of the situation. Now, having chosen life, I began the slow and arduous return to health.

Bhante Gunaratana writes: "A person who loves himself knows what love is and he can share it. You can never give others what you don't have." And Jesus said, "Love thy neighbor as thyself," implying that self-love is the first imperative. Somehow, along the way I had distorted the meaning of service and generosity. I had developed the impression that it was unimportant, even unspiritual and selfish, for me to be self-nurturing or to ask for nurturance from others. I directed all my loving energies outward without thinking about replenishing the source. As beautiful as the feminine devotional impulse to serve is, if the output does not equal the input, it no longer creates health and balance.

The body is the temple of the Spirit. All lofty spiritual ideals, all efforts toward peace on earth, all efforts to heal the environment, to be more kind and loving to our children, our parents, and our mates have their roots in taking care of the body temple through self-love. Self-love is a consideration often neglected by environmentalists, peace advocates, and mothers. We project goodness outside ourselves, thinking that when everything is at last right in the world, when our families are in complete harmony, we will be happy. Since life is in constant flux, the happiness we wait for is constantly eluding us.

When I made the commitment to live, the resources and people I needed to help me get well came trickling in. Apparently the universe had been waiting for me to choose life, waiting at the gate I had erected, ready to offer its riches to me.

First came a doctor who specialized in immune problems. He ran a battery of tests and asked question after probing question.

After studying the results of the tests, he diagnosed me as having chronic fatigue syndrome. He addressed each symptom, one by one. For the massive candida overgrowth, he put me on a special diet and treated me with antifungal medications. He explained that my hypothyroid condition was the result of my body actually attacking its own thyroid gland just as my mind had been attacking itself. For this he prescribed levothyroid. For the virus he prescribed vitamin B_{12} injections and antiviral enzymes. After my body became a little stronger he put me on parasite medication to kill the parasites in my intestines. Out of self-hatred I had vacated my body, and the little creatures had taken over.

How much harder it was to take care of myself once I became a mother! Self-care seemed to fly in the face of the powerful instinct to preserve the species. I always put Nicole first. In Nature the main biological purpose of a life form is to reproduce itself. If the giver of life dies in the process it is no tragedy of Nature because the entity has fulfilled its mission by re-creating itself. But we humans have spiritual missions beyond the preservation of the species, so this natural rule does not strictly apply to us. Yet the instinct to sacrifice ourselves for new life is still present. How often have I seen friends eat the leftovers on their children's plates rather than have a full meal for themselves!

I have some friends who are quite balanced in this regard: They know what their needs are and feel comfortable meeting those needs. But for me it was a struggle to even recognize what my needs were, let alone give myself permission to fulfill them. I got so caught up in working and raising a child alone that I forgot to exercise and rest. I ate on the run and always felt like no matter how much I did, it wasn't enough. I didn't know how desperately I needed a vacation and a more balanced way of life. It didn't occur to me then that my efforts to create more health in the world were jeopardizing my own health! Faced with the reality of my failing health, I had to learn how to eat, to exercise, to breathe, to rest, and to love myself—to take care of myself in real physical ways. Eventually, meeting my needs became instinctual. Taking care of myself became a habit. But in the beginning it took energy to nurture those tiny seeds of self-love and weed out the roots of self-loathing.

I remember the day I came home from the diagnosis having learned that I had chronic fatigue syndrome. I was shocked to discover I had a disease that was considered incurable but relieved to have a name for it. I resolved to do everything I could to become well again. Along with allopathic medications I found an acupuncturist who could treat my symptoms as well as my heart. He was tender and soft, encouraging me to grieve losses I had until then denied. I also went into therapy to grieve the innocence taken from me by early sexual abuse. I would walk into my therapist's office and begin crying, not stopping until the hour was up, then go home and cry some more. It felt as though I had fallen into an endless tunnel of grief and sadness. I had no assurances that I would ever be happy again, but I was committed to following my grief, wherever it led me.

There is a Buddhist meditation practice called Metta, or loving-kindness meditation. I learned this meditation on retreat many years ago and have been practicing it ever since. Sometimes the meditation is short and sometimes it is long, but it always begins with extending loving kindness toward oneself, then toward loved ones, then toward neutral parties, then toward those who push our buttons, then neighbors, all in one's community, country, world, and beyond. When practicing loving-kindness meditation I always begin by saying, "May I be well and happy." Skillful love radiates from the core. When I can love myself, with all of my imperfections, I can love my child, friends, acquaintances, and all beings.

On one winter retreat in Canada I told my teacher during our meditation interview that I was never able to arouse a feeling of love while practicing the loving-kindness meditation. He was puzzled by this and didn't know what to tell me. I went to various American Buddhist communities looking for the healing energy of self-love, but I wasn't finding it. I learned a lot about love from the Buddhist teachings but didn't experience healing love until a friend brought me to his Religious Science church. That community exuded a warmth that attracted me from the start, but it wasn't until years later that I allowed their teachings to help heal me. I was impressed by how this spiritual community embraced all spiritual truths, from any place, culture, or religion, and encouraged their practice. The teachings were eclectic, but the form of prayer Religious Science taught, affirmative prayer, was unlike anything I had ever experienced. I did not grow up with prayer and did not learn about prayer in my Buddhist studies. Affirmative prayer was a totally new practice and way of looking at life for me. It enabled me to heal and connected me with my Divine nature.

I had grown up feeling that life was not safe and that I must struggle to survive emotionally. From Buddhism I learned that life is neutral, not bad or good. From Religious Science I learned that life is good, and that was the pivotal point in my healing. I experienced the feeling of unconditional love from the practitioners who held me when I cried and loved me with their eyes, their arms, their words, and their hearts when I didn't know how to love myself. I learned from the teachings how thought creates our reality. I took a hard look at my own critical thoughts about myself. I was amazed at how self-abusive my thoughts were. I had encountered these thoughts while meditating but had not known how to release them. I learned from the practitioners' guidance and example how to turn negative thoughts into positive, life-affirming ones. As time went on, these new thoughts began creating a new reality. I reprogrammed my thinking, and it changed my entire life. I learned from Buddhism to look within; I learned from Religious Science how to heal the negative trends I found while looking within.

Oddly enough I learned self-love in reverse of the Metta meditation, after feeling the strong love of motherhood. Only then, prompted by my desire to love Nicole better, did I begin learning how to love myself.

The Buddha said, "A mother best serves her child who serves herself." Happiness starts at the smallest unit and radiates outward. As each of us glows with the warmth of self-love, that love radiates to those closest to us, forming a network. We are all interconnected. By first healing myself I have a strong base from which to heal that which is outside me. When I get my thoughts on a loving course, things around me fall into place, creating a domino effect. When we are healthy, everyone around us is stronger; when even one of us is sick, everyone suffers.

Self-love is usually the product of having learned love from our parents. If our parents know how to love us unconditionally, loving ourselves becomes second nature. If our parents were loved, they also know how to love and can pass that love down to their children without even trying. My parents felt love for me in their hearts, but they couldn't teach me what they didn't know, and they didn't know how to love themselves unconditionally, that is, shadow and all. Not many people in our culture know how to give unconditional love, but thankfully it can be learned.

I began learning to love myself by getting to know the self I was loving and doing so without judgment. This meant knowing the self beyond my roles of mother and caretaker, knowing myself as a unique individual with my own mission in life. Homemaking and mothering are what I do but not who I am. There has never been nor will there ever be another person on earth exactly like me. Each one of us is unique and here for a reason. To realize my preciousness and to find my unique mission were my first steps toward self-love. What I began to see was that as I learned to love myself, I naturally and automatically started to take better care of my physical, mental, spiritual, and emotional needs. I needed to bring the awareness of my needs out of the abstract and into the practical realm, where I could actually get those needs met.

Despite any gains in self-acceptance, I still had certain habits I wanted to change, but I worked on changing these habits while accepting my essential self. With self-love I looked at my dark side, feeling the same love and compassion for my unpleasant aspects as I did for my strengths. When I found those negative qualities in myself I took them in like a mother would take in a crying child and cradled them in my arms, stroked their hair, and let them cry their hearts out in a warm, safe place.

When a child acts out there's always a reason. Children don't act out because they're *bad*. You may not be able to find out what the problem is. Sometimes it clears up by itself, sometimes it takes effort and analysis to get to the bottom of it, but there is always an underlying cause. Just knowing that there is a reason for any unpleasant behavior helps me to not react so strongly. Negative behavior is a form of communication. The question is "What is being said?"

Just as one of the first ways a mother shows love for her newborn is by attending to its physical needs, we begin our practice of healthy self-love by taking care of our own physical needs. In Maslow's theory of the hierarchy of needs, survival, food, and shelter are at the base. In order to achieve mental, emotional, and spiritual balance, basic physical needs must be met first. You don't teach hungry children how to read; you feed them first. Otherwise they will be preoccupied with their basic survival needs.

When I became a mother finding time to exercise was challenging. I was always running around, lifting things, pushing and pulling, and reaching for things. That's not the same as swimming ten laps or dancing or aerobics or running or any other rhythmically consistent movement. When I became a foster mother of a newborn baby, Marie, it became even more difficult to set aside the time to exercise. After a few weeks of staying home without any exercise I began taking long walks with the baby wrapped up in a baby carrier tied snugly against my chest and rediscovered the joy of walking. Henry David Thoreau said, "An early morning walk is a blessing for the whole day."

Early in the morning, late in the afternoon, and sometimes in the evening I would put Marie in the baby carrier, and off we would go for a walk. As we walked I drank in the smells of wood smoke from our neighbors' fireplaces and anise from the side of the road. I heard the woodpeckers and mockingbirds and sparrows and barking dogs. I saw cats luxuriating under trees and on the tops of cars. I passed joggers and said hello to neighbors. I savored this time to think, and when I got lost in my thoughts a breeze through the eucalyptus trees would wake me up to the moment. Jean-Jacques Rousseau said, "Never have I thought so much, never have I realized my own existence so much, never have I been so much alive than when walking."

Whether I am in the city, with its window displays and people and interesting buildings, or in the country, with its trees and fresh air and creatures, walking brings me closer to my environment, and to myself, far better than any other form of exercise. You can walk in the country or in the city; it's free, and you can do it alone or with a baby strapped to your back, or even with toddlers on bikes or in strollers.

In movement I can play and enjoy my body. Sometimes I get so caught up in the details of everyday life that I neglect the child within me. I forget to play, to be spontaneous, to just be there without *doing* anything *productive*. When I walk, the wonder child in me comes out to play. Play has no practical goal, yet the playful child within holds the key to joy and wonder. I don't need to give up my childlike nature because I am an adult, a parent. On the contrary, the more active and alive my inner child is, the more I am able to understand the heart and mind of my child. My inner child makes everyday life more fun and surprising. Today exercise is a high priority in my life. Just as I carve out the time to finish a budget or get Nicole to soccer practice, I now carve out the time to exercise. I'm not much good to anybody if I don't honor my basic needs.

Another need that is so basic to living that I have tended to take it for granted is breathing. Fresh, clean air that is free from formaldehyde, smog, petrofumes, and other pollutants has a powerful healing effect. Learning to breath deeply rather than shallowly cleans out the lungs, thereby activating the lymph system, which transports the toxins out of our bodies. Deep breathing says a heartfelt yes to life. When I described my symptoms of fatigue to my spiritual teacher he told me I should be careful with my diet, exercise at least fifteen minutes a day, and practice deep breathing and relaxation three times a day. I went home and practiced deep breathing. It has greatly increased my vitality.

Once I learned how to care for my basic physical needs I began turning up the volume on my well-being. I began to give my body treats as a way of expressing self-love: taking a hot bath with candlelight and music to relax after a long day, taking a hike at the ocean and breathing in the beautiful sea air, or soaking up the colors of the mountains and flowers. We all have our special places, our green hills or rose gardens. Finding those places and indulging in the joy of being in a human body on a green-and-blue planet replenishes the strength I need to deal with whatever life may hand me.

One subtle yet basic aspect of self-love I have learned is to honor my need for solitude. As a householder I am bombarded with many stresses and strains throughout the day. I had to learn to carve out time to be alone and recenter myself, to drink in the silence, to not have anybody needing anything from me, to just be myself in a quiet place. Anne Morrow Lindbergh's book *Gift from the Sea,* speaks beautifully about women's need for solitude. She wrote: "The artist knows he must be alone to create; the writer to work out his thoughts; the musician to compose; the saint to pray. But women need solitude in order to find again the true essence of themselves: that firm strand which will be the indispensable center of a whole web of human relationships. She must find that inner stillness which Charles Morgan describes as 'the stilling of the soul within the activities of the mind and body so that it might be still as the axis of a revolving wheel is still.'"

When my mother had three small children she would wake up at 5:30 in the morning to meditate and center herself. It was her saving grace. In the wee small hours of the morning when all was still and quiet she would have the house to herself. Being all alone during these moments, she could reconnect with her inner self. As a child I remember lying in bed, somehow sensing that this was my mother's time, burrowing back down under the covers so as not to disturb her. When I got out of bed and pattered into the living room I smelled incense and felt the peace that solitude brings reflected in my mother's eyes.

When you have been giving all day you need to come back to your source and reconnect, recharge. This was such a valuable lesson for me. If I failed to create time to be alone I sometimes became resentful of my child and friends. I sometimes got to a point of being there physically but not emotionally. Whenever I nourished myself I returned to my family much more present. After a session of solitude I could come back to Nicole and really hear her. If Nicole came to me with her problems when I felt overloaded with work and hadn't taken some quiet space for myself, I might tell her, "I don't know. You figure it out." Mothers everywhere are confronted with dilemmas like this. It's not that we don't love our children or care about their problems; it's just that we have nothing left to give at that moment. When I was married I spent every Friday by myself. My husband would take Nicole for the day, which was great for their relationship, and I would be free to do as I pleased. There are ways to find time to be alone. Pioneer women who worked from early morning till late at night found their solitude in their sewing and praying. When you have ten children you catch your time alone where you can, even in the midst of your work.

I have a friend who shares child care with another mom. One day she takes the children, and another day her friend takes them. I have another friend who needs a couple of hours alone at night. Her children go to bed at 8:30 sharp. It has always amazed me how they go to bed at that time without question. Once they are tucked away in their beds, their mother sorts her laundry, watches TV, and ferociously protects that alone time like a lioness.

Another need every woman has is the need to create. The most contented mothers I know are the ones who have interests apart from mothering and householding. Nurturing our dreams feeds every other part of our lives. When I follow my star and stay true to my purpose in this life I am a model of happiness and easily pass that happiness down to my family.

Mothers also need nurturing friendships. A child can't possibly provide us with the mental stimulation and emotional support that other adults provide. It's important to create and maintain relationships with peers, to find friends with whom we can share our thoughts and feelings, our joys and sorrows, a good meal. I don't know where I'd be without my friends. As women everywhere have discovered, friends help us believe in ourselves when we bottom out and listen to us when we feel excited, angry, lonely, and puzzled. At times when we stumble into the dark pits of our psyches, friends are there to shine a light so we can find our way out. When Ananda, the Buddha's chief attendant, asked the Buddha if friendship was an important part of the spiritual path, the Buddha said, "It is not an important part of the spiritual path, it *is* the spiritual path." You may fall into the pit alone, but you can make it out with the love and support of kindred spirits.

Sometimes I hit a problem that neither my friends nor family are skilled enough to help me with. At such times taking care of myself also means seeking professional help. Just knowing that I don't have to solve every problem all by myself, that there are people who are skilled in listening and reflecting back what they see and hear with honesty and caring, makes solving problems more of an engaging journey than a frightening abyss. The right therapist or rabbi or monk or priest or practitioner can help shed light on the conflict and help develop understanding of what is going on much more rapidly than I can by toughing it out by myself.

Feeling gratitude for the richness of life and finding my unique place in that richness is an essential aspect of self-love. Reading, hearing talks, and joining with others who share my values help me harvest the richness. Whether it be by going to church or temple or a meditation retreat, I nourish myself by joining with kindred spirits. Knowing my path and meeting with others who can support me on it is essential for the spiritual journey.

The church or temple has traditionally been a place where women can find their solitude and experience their spirituality. I went on seven-day silent retreats once a year to join with other meditators and reaffirm my spiritual purpose. I came back to my mothering and homemaking with a stronger spiritual intent in all I did. Now I go to church each Sunday. It is a time to spiritually recharge and to laugh and cry with my community. That connectedness sustains me throughout the week. When I leave my home to get spiritually nourished I get an overview of my processes and bring a heightened spiritual perspective back to my family.

The middle path avoids the extremes of indulgence and neglect. As mothers we all need to learn to consciously strike a balance between our own needs and those of our families without getting lost in our needs or in the needs of others. When we focus on taking care of everybody but ourselves we easily get resentful, depleted, and burnt out. If we only take care of ourselves we lose connectedness. By neglecting self-love we teach our children to neglect themselves when they become parents.

Self-love is now the very heart of my mental and physical health care. Practicing this caring attitude toward myself has proved to be an investment in my future and that of my friends and family. It requires mapping out my needs and following that map, it also requires self-discipline. As the discipline bears fruit, it becomes easier to stick to a self-care program. Exercise, taking the time to eat mindfully, carving out time for solitude and play, for friends, for meditation or prayer—all take a degree of planning. I have come to a heartfelt realization that I deserve to be happy, that it is not a selfish thing to take care of myself but rather the best thing I can do for my family and the world.

Now I am back in the world singing, writing, and taking care of my family. The experience of descending to the depths of my pain, anger, and fear, and bringing them back up into the light has made me a deeper, richer person. I am grateful for the wisdom I've gained on this arduous journey. It is not something I would choose or wish for anyone, yet surprisingly it has been one of the greatest blessings in my life.

UNCONDITIONAL LOVE ✐

Skillful Loving

Love is a fruit in season at all times, and within reach of every hand. Anyone may gather it and no limit is set. Everyone can reach this love through meditation, spirit of prayer, and sacrifice by an intense inner life.

MOTHER TERESA

I still remember that miraculous moment when Nicole's fragile wet body was placed on mine and I felt the gates of my heart swing open. Even though I was completely exhausted, I wanted to gaze forever at this baby's ancient face. I walked through the valley of death while bringing her into this world, and there she was, my beloved, my old friend, my buddy.

For the next several months my heart was like an open wound. Tears filled my eyes at the simple falling of a leaf. I had left the world of time and schedules. I was living in feminine time, the here and now, and the immediate moment was all that was real to me. The hormones filling my body relaxed me, encouraging me to nurse my baby and ensure her existence. On the one hand, I felt like the most wondrous being in all the world, the first Madonna performing the miracle of bringing forth life from my womb and pushing that life out into the air and light of the earth. On the other hand, I felt like a common woman, like women everywhere whose bodies have served as vessels for the miracle of birth.

I reentered the world of linear time immensely curious about other women's experiences of birthing and early motherhood. I wondered whether or not my transformative experience was unique. Looking around me at friends who had recently become mothers, I saw hardened faces becoming softer and soft faces becoming radiant during those early months after they had given birth to their children.

In giving birth I experienced for the first time in my life the magic of a love that was truly unconditional. Suddenly I was holding a being for whom I would give my life, no questions asked, simply because she existed and was in my keeping. She was so vulnerable and needed me so completely that I was touched to the very roots of my tenderness.

Sai Baba wrote: "The aim of all spiritual practice is love." What a divine gift my insight into unconditional love was! It was a fitting and just reward for the literal self-sacrifice of pregnancy and the grueling trial of labor. But, as with any other insight, it gradually fades into the background unless it is nourished and developed. I saw women for whom this insight led to boundless love for all beings. I saw other women who forgot that we are responsible for all children, and devoted themselves solely to their own.

It felt so good to be in love with my new baby that I wanted this oceanic feeling to last forever, to grow to include everything I came into contact with. However, the glow faded, as all things do, leaving me with a hunger for its return. I felt a growing fatigue as the day-to-day necessities of mothering and homemaking asserted themselves, and the glow became a memory. I poured over every book on love that I could find, from current self-help books to ancient teachings, looking outside myself for something that was closer than my breath. Then, as I was cleaning out some old papers at the bottom of a drawer, I came across a booklet my teacher Anagarika had given me called "The Practice of Lovingkindness," by Nanmoli Thera. There I found exactly what I needed to know to begin my journey toward the understanding of love.

As I turned the pages of this seemingly arcane pamphlet, I found the clearest definition of love's varied faces I had ever seen. In it the Buddha spoke lucidly about a subject that most teachings I had encountered had alluded to yet had often left to lofty fantasy, the subject of love. I was thrilled to find love articulated in such a concise manner. The teachings began with the premise that the word *love* is used to cover a multitude of distinct and varied feelings. The Buddha broke the feelings down into two principle modes: (1) the love of lovers, passionate, consuming love—Eros, and (2) the love of a mother toward her child, unconditional love, agape. Buddha took the latter as the basis for his teachings concerning universal love.

I had been aware of the distinction between Eros and agape for some time but was fascinated to discover how the Buddha further divided unconditional love into four categories: *metta,* or loving kindness, which is being a true friend in need; *karuna,* which is compassion for another's suffering; *mudita,* which is sympathetic joy or gladness at another's happiness; and *upekkha,* which is onlooking equanimity, loving detachment. What an aid to my understanding of love these categories proved to be! They made clear for me concepts I had only partially grasped before, mainly that love is not an abstract and magical property with which only certain lucky people are blessed but a depth of experience that can be cultivated with practice.

The Buddha explained that every form of love has a direct enemy and an indirect enemy. An indirect enemy is something that looks very much like love but is tinged with what the Buddha called unwholesome states of mind, such as ignorance or egocentric intent. A direct enemy of love is a mind state that is its direct opposite, such as hate. It is not possible for love to exist in the same mind state as its direct opposite.

The first of the four forms of love the Buddha described, metta, or loving kindness, can be expressed by friendship, by respecting who my child is, as an individual distinct and separate from me. The Vietnamese word for children means happiness. It is this loving kindness I feel whenever my child and I are just being friends. I remember when Nicole was fourteen years old and came home one day with green hair. My first impulse, when I looked at what appeared to be a tangle of seaweed thrown haphazardly on top of my daughter's once beautiful blond hair, was to judge her. By then I had learned the hard way to choose my battles carefully. I developed the practice of asking myself if any harm had been done to her body, mind, or spirit. Truthfully answering no to each, I said, "Come here, let me look more closely at your hair." She came over to the couch where I had been reading. I sat up and stroked her hair gently. In the next few moments I felt her body relax as I loved her without words. Judgment faded as I realized that this was what she needed to do to assert her individuality. I now began to see the creativity and fun of her dyed hair once I got past my blind judgment.

Loving kindness has included listening and reading to Nicole, feeding her, driving her to school, laughing at her knock-knock jokes even after she tells them for the fiftieth time, braiding her hair, disciplining her, and putting a little surprise in her lunch box. Parenting with loving kindness is thoughtful parenting, but it is also playful parenting. I feel so much joy, so light, when I interact with Nicole in a playful, friendly way.

Loving kindness is the practice of looking squarely at other people and loving them in spite of their human frailties. There's a wonderful Arabian proverb that says, "A friend is one to whom one may pour out all the contents of one's heart, chaff and grain together, knowing that the gentlest of hands will take and sift it, keep what is worth keeping and, with a breath of kindness, blow the rest away." The book *The Wind in the Willows* beautifully illustrates how creatures can be friends and look out for one another in spite of incessant transgressions. Mr. Toad is a boastful, impulsive, arrogant beast and yet his fellow river dwellers remain his staunch supporters. Rejecting him isn't even an option; they are friends.

One day, when Nicole was angry with everything and everyone, including me, she looked me in the eye and yelled, "I hate you." I was hurt and shocked and felt angry and sorry for myself. I was able to take a deep breath into my hurt heart and tell Nicole that I needed a time-out. Instead of lashing back at her, which was my first reaction, I stood there in my vulnerability. After taking some time to feel my feelings I remembered how other mothers had told me about the times their children said "I hate you." It softened the blow somewhat to know that it wasn't only my child who said these things. As the shock subsided I was able to remember how powerless children can feel and how words are sometimes their only way to release psychic toxins. Instead of creating even more toxins by reacting with my own anger, I was able to be present in my hurt and even to become more powerful through the realization that my emotions need not be at the mercy of every wind that blows. At the same time my actions were teaching Nicole how to respond rather than react.

When I radiate metta while teaching, I transmit a joy of learning to Nicole. When I model social skills that will be helpful in negotiating a world that is complex and more conditional in its acceptance than I am, I transmit caring. I taught Nicole to say please and thank you, to bring her dishes to the sink, and to not interrupt. I taught her these skills not because I need her to be a certain way in order for me to love her, but because I want her to feel the love of others and move gracefully into the world.

With loving kindness I practice really listening to Nicole. I see who she is and want her to find full expression for her own unique self. Nicole is quite different from me. She is more extroverted and loves to be with people, whereas I love to be alone with my paintbrush or guitar. In many ways I have had to listen carefully to understand her needs because they are so different from mine. When a friend of hers died she asked if she could have a bunch of friends over for a party. I deal with grief by turning inward, while she needed her friends around her to get loud with, to cry with, to both escape and face the painful reality of her friend's death. By avoiding the trap of thinking that my way was the *right* way I expressed the loving kindness that she needed at that time.

Seeking a deeper understanding of loving kindness, I read that the indirect enemy of metta is selfish attachment. As humans we have a tendency to possess and cling to that which brings us happiness. It's there in the jealousy of lovers, in a mother's feeding off her child's accomplishments. It's human, and we all do it. I have a friend who lives through her children's accomplishments. She doesn't have her own spiritual practice or career or even a hobby that she is passionate about. She takes everything her children do personally, and so the children feel they do not have the psychic space to make their own mistakes, make their own life choices, and learn from these choices in a free and nonthreatening way. Every mistake the children make on their own learning journeys causes their mother great pain, and neither can they fully enjoy their own accomplishments since she is always there to take credit for each success. A keen interest in her children looks like love. In truth, there is an undercurrent of selfish attachment. I noticed that same tendency in myself when I watched as Nicole was putting off going to college. I became aware of feeling uncomfortable when my friends questioned me about what Nicole was doing. Part of me wanted her to go to college so that I would look good. I had to remember that when I love unselfishly I put my beloved's interests first and trust the process she will go through to make the choices that are consistent with who she is.

Again the Buddha teaches that the direct enemy of metta is hatred. Loving kindness and hatred cannot coexist in our minds. One afternoon I came home from work after one of my students had yelled at me. While she yelled at me, I held my feelings inside. When I came home I was still in a lot of turmoil. I was walking around with a dark cloud over me as I made Nicole's dinner and helped her with her homework. When I tucked her into bed that night she said, "Do you hate me?" I was shocked! Nothing was further from the truth. I told her I loved her and that I was sorry but that I had been having a difficult day. There was a great lesson in this for me. When we're feeling angry, those closest to us usually get the fallout from our anger. We don't do this consciously, but children feel the anger radiating from us just the same, and it crowds out the love we feel for them. Children are especially vulnerable to this since it is natural for them to feel that they are somehow responsible for everything in their world.

The second of the four forms of love named by the Buddha is karuna, or compassion. Karuna is an openhearted awareness of suffering. The Sufi teacher Dard wrote: "Misery and joy have the same shape in this world: you may call the rose an open heart or a broken heart." Sometimes I try to protect myself from the pain of loving by closing my heart to "others." This creates the illusion of duality and separation. When my heart is closed the light of happiness is also shut out, and the pain of this constriction becomes a vague depression. Keeping our hearts open, even to the point where they are pierced and aching, is a truly courageous and necessary practice for anyone on the path of love.

Sometimes it's easier to project compassion outside myself, and the further outside the better. It is easier to have compassion for the starving children in Africa than to have compassion for my neighbor, who, in his loneliness, riddles me with complaints, or for myself, when I yell at Nicole because I just can't take it anymore.

Since becoming a mother I've really needed to learn to have compassion for myself. People readily offer their opinion of how I am raising my child, yet I have been my own worst critic, using the criticism of others as ammunition to attack myself. I have needed to become firm in my resolve to listen to others but to ultimately follow my own intuition. Any unskillful actions or thoughts I have stem from a lack of insight into the true nature of things. I am growing, and as I grow I make mistakes in order to learn. Feeling anger, feeling needy, feeling inadequate are all a part of the dance of growth. We continually need to forgive ourselves, to have compassion for ourselves, and to soften so that we can grow from our mistakes rather than be burdened by them.

Accepting my own imperfections as natural and human has helped me develop karuna. It has opened the door to understanding and accepting others who have their own pain and their own struggles. Mother Teresa said, "We know that if we really want to love we must learn how to forgive." In learning to forgive myself I learn to forgive others. Speaking hastily and out of excitement one afternoon, I told Nicole that we could go to the beach the next weekend. What I didn't do was look at my calendar, and when I finally did I saw that I had other commitments that day. I had to renege on my promise, and Nicole was understandably and justifiably angry and disappointed. I had made a mistake. I had broken a promise to my beloved child. Not only did I need to make amends to Nicole, I needed to forgive myself for my human error.

When I feel hurt by another adult and have trouble forgiving her, I try to imagine how it was for her when she was a child.

When you look beyond the surface, you can see that people hurt others because they are themselves in pain. They learned about causing pain from things that happened to them when they were children, vulnerable and unable to defend themselves. Feeling unsafe to express their pain, they internalized it, locked it up inside their bodies, where it lay in wait to emerge at the least provocation. One day when Nicole was a teenager I came home with an award for writing and proudly placed it in front of my mother. She responded by bringing out awards that she had received in the past. I felt hurt and angry. My moment of victory, which I had wanted to share with my mother, had been stolen.

In retrospect, I can see that my mother grew up in a home where there had been a scarcity of attention for the children. She got what little attention she could by being smart and by bringing home awards that proved her worth. I can now see the situation from my mother's perspective and can release any resentment I've been holding on to. In order to move on from hurt to a place where I am compassionate and nurturing rather than create more pain, I need to forgive myself and those around me over and over again. It is only by doing this that we can live and love in the present.

When Nicole came home from school in tears one afternoon saying that the children called her names I felt her anguish. I remembered when I was a child and other children teased me. This sympathetic pain is at the heart of karuna. I could feel Nicole's pain because I was willing to remember that same feeling in myself. By staying vulnerable to these difficult feelings I can give the gift of compassion to others. I stay vulnerable by remembering that I am not the fleeting emotions that ripple on the surface of my consciousness; I am the deep ocean undulating peacefully underneath the disturbances. I can endure feelings of hurt. Feelings do not have the power to alter the diamond jewel of my true self in any way.

The near enemy of compassion is pity. When I feel pity I am remaining separate and unmoved by the person before me who is in pain. With compassion I feel, "Oh yes. I can touch that part of my heart and it really hurts." When I keep my heart closed with pity I withhold the nourishment my friend needs for her healing process to unfold and delay my own healing as well. Sir Thomas Browne wrote: "By compassion we make others' misery our own, and so, by relieving them, we relieve ourselves also." The greatest healers I've known are those who have lived through much pain in their lives and have been able to transform that pain into compassion rather than bitterness. I develop more compassion for the suffering of others when I remember how much energy and resolve it takes for me to pull out of a downward spiral and remain aware of how my own pain feels.

I have a dear friend who has been a foster mother to many children. She is truly a spiritual hero and model for compassionate mothering. She survived an abusive childhood. She is particularly skillful with children who have been abused, as so many foster children have been. The pain she suffered from her abuse could have gone one of two ways: She could have become bitter and abusive herself. Instead, she chose to face her pain and stop the cycle of abuse by helping others stuck in that cycle. Through her spiritual faith and practice she developed the courage and strength to transform her pain into compassion. She is able to relate extremely well to children who are filled with fear and to give them the space they need to open up to her love. She knows from experiencing her own pain and fear that their acting out is coming from the hurt they need to express in order to heal their traumatized psyches. She has learned to be patient and nonjudgmental, to love the children in her care unconditionally, just as they are in the moment. She knows in her heart what an abused child needs in order to feel trust and hope again. Her own greatest anguish became the key to her greatest gift.

The direct enemy of compassion is cruelty. When we cut ourselves off from another's heart, cruelty has a fertile field in which to grow. When our hearts are in touch with the hearts of others we are unable to act with cruelty. I've watched children on the playground taunt and bully more vulnerable children. What compels these children to hurt another child? It takes looking honestly and courageously at ourselves to unearth the seeds of cruelty. I remember that when I was in high school I said cruel things about a girl who was less popular than I. Now that my heart is cleaner I can see that I used that girl to build up my own sagging self-confidence. She became an object, not a person, to me. Cruelty stems from objectifying another, from losing touch with the connectedness of all things.

From the moment my baby came out of the womb I was confronted with her suffering. Even though I strived to make her birth as gentle as possible, simply being thrust into a world that at best did not compare to the comfort of the all-encompassing womb was a source of suffering. My baby was hungry—I felt her suffering. My baby was alone for the first time, no longer connected to my body—I felt her suffering. This is an example of the Buddha's first noble truth, the truth of dukka, or life is suffering. We are all subject to dis-ease; we all will die. It is not within my power to create a world that is free from all suffering for my child or for me. I can, however, keep my heart open to her sufferings and let her know that she is not alone, that I am standing by her, and that I love her. When I stop resisting the reality of suffering it is easier to flow with the natural way of things, and the great burden of trying to create a world free of suffering is lifted.

When I am teaching compassion by example I am able to teach Nicole that suffering exists alongside joy. It is all part of life. I had to face this lesson when my marriage dissolved. The breakup of our family was devastating for Nicole. There's no way around it: Divorce creates a tear in the fabric of our children's hearts. Even though Nicole's father and I parted as friends, it caused Nicole great pain. I spent many years feeling guilty about this. Now I see that Nicole became stronger in the broken parts by feeling her pain and moving through it with awareness. She then could be a loving compassionate presence for her friends when they were faced with trauma. I wonder if she would be able to meet them, heart to heart, as skillfully as she does if she hadn't gone through her own trauma and healing. When we overprotect our children we unwittingly teach them that suffering is bad, thereby inhibiting their growth of karuna and setting them up to resist anything unpleasant. How much more skillful it is to stay with our children and love them through their hard times rather than try to make a perfect world for them!

If we allow it to, motherhood can connect us with the rest of humanity. Acknowledging suffering can open us to the realization that all of us suffer the pain of loving. Compassion deepens and expands, cutting across cultural barriers and going straight to the heart of the common human predicament. If a mother loses a child, does it matter if she is Chinese, African, American, or Lebanese? The feeling is the same for every mother.

The third form of love, mudita, or sympathetic joy, is the joy I felt when Nicole took her first step, turned around, and looked at me, all excited, as I beamed with surprise. I felt sympathetic joy when Nicole was older and swung herself way up high on the backyard swing, flying to the tops of the trees. One morning Nicole was late for school. I went in to her room to see what the matter was and found her crawling under her bed. I asked her what she was doing, and she told me she had lost her favorite rock. Down we went, among unpaired socks and pieces of puzzles and candy wrappers, both on the same mission, to find the lost rock. After about five minutes she shrieked with joy! She had found her rock, and we both glowed with a sense of accomplishment and camaraderie. What a wonderful moment that was for both of us! Mudita is a pure shining happiness. It feels like a warm glow or a bright light from within. It is one of the great rewards of parenting, undefinable and totally delightful!

By expressing joy and sharing such happy moments with our children we help them to appreciate the possibilities for joy in their lives. Joy is infectious and far more powerful than negativity. I didn't used to think of joy as something that could be practiced. I used to think of it as something that I was either graced with or stuck without. I have come to realize that loving is not always inspired by our environments and neither is joy. Sometimes it takes conscious effort on our parts to become joyful. In *The Way of Splendor,* Edward Hoffman writes about a wise rabbi who said, "Always be joyful, no matter what you are . . . with happiness you give a person life. Everyday . . . we must deliberately induce in ourselves a buoyant, exuberant attitude toward life, in this manner, we gradually become receptive to the subtle mysteries around us. And if no inspired moments come, we should act as though we have them anyway. . . . If you have no enthusiasm put up a front. Act enthusiastic and the feeling will become genuine." And the Torah says, "Act and you will become."

There was a time in my life when misery was a habit. Misery can be very seductive, after all. For many years I had to remind myself that misery is only one aspect of the human experience; joy is another. Any view of life that excludes either suffering or joy is incomplete. When I saw the Dalai Lama I was struck not only by his brilliance and compassion for the suffering of others but also by his buoyancy and joy. You can see the level of development of an individual if you observe how fully they express joy. Kalu Rimpoche, Ananda Mitreya, and other transcendent beings I have been fortunate to meet, glow with joy.

Sometimes, when I am feeling miserable and I cross paths with someone who is feeling happy, I become irritated with him and sarcastic about his happiness. This irritation, or jealousy, is the direct enemy of sympathetic joy. To experience sympathetic joy I need to first get in touch with the mudita, or sympathetic joy, that I feel for myself. I can only share what I have already given myself.

The indirect but insidious enemy of sympathetic joy is our attachment to that joy. When I want that delicious joy to go on forever I sometimes try to cage it, to pretend that everything is just peachy, denying the dark aspect of life. I know I'm doing this when I clench my teeth as I smile and say that everything is great. That kind of "love" is a smoke screen. Children sense this right away and usually see right through us. When I allow joy to come and go instead of becoming attached to it, I save myself needless suffering.

Sympathetic joy makes the difficulties of parenting more bearable and everyday life more full of fun, more surprising, and more deeply rewarding. There is always a full range of emotions from which to choose. There are injustices I can choose to be angry about; there are things I want but don't have that I can choose to be unhappy about; and there is beauty all around me that I can choose to be delighted by. Happiness is a choice. There is an infinitely abundant picture in front of us at all times, and our free will gives us the power to choose to focus on virtually any part of it. This is the greatest power we will ever possess.

The fourth and last form of love the Buddha defined is the most subtle, the most profound, and the least understood. It is upekkha, or *onlooking equinimity*. This form of love cannot be cultivated without a strong base of the other three forms, and so it is the last to be defined. Upekkha is the ability to observe struggles, joys, and all other states of mind with open and loving detachment. Upekkha comes from the realization that pain is a part of growth, part of the human condition. It is the courage to look on lovingly at that which we cannot change.

No matter how much I love my child, parenting is not always a pretty picture. By the time my daughter was fourteen years old she was totally out of control. Many factors contributed to this: years of unresolved pain over her parents' divorce, abandonment by her father, a dysfunctional school system, and a mother who was distracted by the struggle to survive. At fourteen her world exploded. I hadn't a clue as to how I could help her stop the downward spiral she was in. Although I didn't know where to turn to help heal my child, I was one hundred percent committed to her well-being. I searched for an alternative and finally found a boarding school that specialized in children who were at risk. The school could give her the special attention she needed, but it turned out to not be enough. One day the headmaster called to tell me Nicole was threatening to run away and that I needed to come get her. I was facing one of the greatest dilemmas of my life. I knew that if I let her come home, I would be teaching her that threats work, yet the school would not keep her.

When everything I can consciously come up with falls short, the best thing I can do is surrender. It is through the opening I created by releasing my ego, that a third alternative appeared—a twenty-one-day wilderness program in Idaho. I had one day to make the decision whether or not to send her there, find the considerable funds to pay for it, and figure out how to get her from Utah to Idaho against her will. Step by step the universe supported my resolve to lift my child up. I made the commitment, and the pieces fell into place. I told the headmaster to put Nicole on a plane with a chaperone, and then, en route to Idaho, she was told that she was going to a wilderness program in Idaho. This was one of the hardest things I've ever had to do as a mother. I sent my distressed child into the wilderness in the middle of one of the coldest winters on record to find the lost parts of her self.

While she was gone I kept a lit candle in the window with her picture taped to the glass candleholder. I prayed every day and stayed with her in consciousness. I read the parenting book they sent me from Idaho and opened to my part of this healing process. I became aware of the changes I needed to make in my parenting. At the end of the twenty-one days I flew to Idaho and met Nicole at the trail's end. There, over the snow-covered hills hiked ten children who had touched bottom and found that they could survive. Dirty from three weeks of living out of a backpack, heart open and vulnerable, she looked me in the eye, and I knew my girl was back. For the first time since she was four years old she was walking without a chip on her shoulder. We embraced, said goodbye to Idaho, and drove back to Utah together so that she could finish out her year at school.

On the ride to Utah Nicole thanked me for sending her to Idaho. She talked nonstop for hours, a minor miracle considering that previously she communicated only in grunts and monosyllables. She told me about how she had learned that there are always numerous points of view. She shared her point of view, asked me what mine was—another minor miracle—and then she shared with me the concept of the third point of view, the eagle-eye point of view. She explained, as we drove through the naked brown and white landscape, how important it is to look at a situation from above to get a long-range perspective on it. It was one of the most intimate and enlightening few hours I have ever spent with another person. I learned a lot from Nicole on that car ride, and she felt empowered as she taught me what she had learned.

If I had wanted just to get rid of her and have someone else solve my problem, I would have acted with cold detachment when I sent her to Idaho, but my heart was fully engaged, more attuned to her than ever before. With a deep, active love in my heart—tough love—I let my beloved child face the fire of initiation as an act of equanimity.

Tough love demands letting our children experience the consequences without interfering but with deep love in our hearts. Without authentic unconditional affection and love, tough love can easily become cold detachment, equanimity's near enemy. The difference between equanimity and detachment can be difficult to detect. Equanimity involves heartfelt objectivity whereas detachment is its antithesis, a cold dispassion that causes the one who remains detached and those who come into contact with that person a great amount of suffering and alienation. Equanimity requires a loving and open heart. I needed to be willing to go through the fire with Nicole, without interfering with her process. By doing so, we were both profoundly healed as we grew and expanded our capacity to love. Six years later Nicole is still filled with self-esteem and self-love.

Equanimity implies a mental balance and an evenness of temperament. It is the quality of being calm and at peace. Equanimity keeps me from getting caught up in all the emotions that surround me in my everyday life. I am finding equanimity to be one of the jewels of maturity. It has taken living through many winters and watching spring pass and return again and again to not lose myself in mourning when the trees lose their leaves. It is the wisdom that comes not only from surviving pain but also from emerging stronger and wiser from each difficult encounter.

Now, when I find myself in difficult situations, I say, "What can I learn from this?" Rather than rejecting the pain I welcome it, knowing there are gifts tucked within its thorny folds.

It is with upekkha that as young mothers we look at our toddlers' frustrations over not being able to walk or talk, and feel their pain even as we keep hands off, realizing these challenges are important aspects of their development. I've learned not to try to take Nicole's pain from her; that's how she develops the muscles necessary for her own quest, and I do not want to take that from her. When I try to make things better for Nicole, it is often not for her sake but for easing my own discomfort at feeling so helpless as she suffers. But that is not love. It is overprotectiveness, which can be quite destructive. It's not easy to watch a child in pain and remain still and aware with love in your heart. A mother's helplessness in the face of her loved one's pain certainly makes her want to shut off her feelings. To remain open when we most want to close down is a high art to master. We must give ourselves a long lead with this lesson and just keep practicing.

The indirect enemy of equanimity is emotional attachment, which appears in the form of passion. When Nicole was in a school play there was a little girl whose mother was fighting the director, trying to convince him that her daughter was the most talented of all the children in the class and deserved a particular part. As the mother passionately argued her point, her little girl looked on in shame and embarrassment. It was clear that the girl who had already been given the part was well suited to the role, but this berating mother was blinded by her passionate attachment. When we are passionately attached to our children we cannot see them clearly. They become extensions of ourselves, and we lose all sense of clear boundaries. How sad it is that through our passionate attachment we suffocate our children with "love." Love never suffocates; passionate attachment does.

At its core a mother's love is unconditional. When Nicole does something I don't like I may get angry, but I never stop loving her. My love is without question or reason. This is the kind of love that nurtures self-esteem, and it is the single most important element of a child's growth and development. Mother Teresa says, "People today are hungry for love, for understanding love which is the only answer to loneliness and great poverty." In my human unskillfulness I sometimes forget to express the unconditionality of my love. It is easy to get wrapped up in the drama of the moment and forget to let Nicole know that I accept her just the way she is. Expressing love is a wonderful habit to cultivate. It has become an everyday practice for Nicole and me. We have learned to end each good-bye with the simple yet powerful words "I love you."

ATTACHMENT ✎

Bonding and Releasing

> Your children are not your children. They are the sons and daughters of life's longing for itself. They come through you but not from you, and though they are with you yet they belong not to you.

> KAHLIL GIBRAN, *The Prophet*

As a Buddhist practitioner I have committed my life to the study and practice of love. As a mother I have become entwined in love's flowers and love's thorns. The more time I spend loving, the more I learn about love's dark sister, grief. As mothering deepens my capacity to love and be loved, I become more attuned to the pain of sister grief. I have come to recognize her by the heavy touch on the exact spot that love once touched so lightly.

One day at about 4:30 in the afternoon, I was sitting in my office surrounded by blue walls and scraps of scribbled-on paper. I had just completed a budget that would enable me to write throughout the winter without worrying about money. I was feeling smugly organized and was just about to brew my afternoon tea when the phone rang. It was Joyce, a foster-care case worker at social services. I had recently become a licensed emergency shelter caregiver. Nicole was nine years old, and we both wanted more children in our lives. Becoming a foster home seemed like a good way to make this happen. Joyce said, "I have a four-day-old baby that needs emergency shelter. Can you come pick her up?" I told her I would, and forty-five minutes later I was the foster mom of a five-pound, four-ounce premature baby girl.

Marie was tiny when I brought her to my home, a home that hadn't seen a baby in nine years. I had no bassinet, no changing table, or baby thermometer, or diapers, or breast milk. She arrived with some diapers, some bottled milk, and one of those sad black garbage bags containing the remnants of the foster child's former life. We fed her and changed her diapers until it was time for bed. After settling in I climbed into my queen-sized bed with Marie and went to sleep.

Marie slept tight up against my body. My instincts told me she needed the warmth and life force that my body offered. She felt my breathing and I felt hers. Every few hours she would squirm and make an "ooo" shape with her little rosebud lips to tell me she was hungry. I would go get the bottle and feed her, then go back to sleep. How sweet she felt, so still and peaceful against my body. We were exchanging a warmth, a cozy protection.

The weeks went on and I became more adept at making bottles. I had breast-fed Nicole and was surprised at how Marie continued to thrive on the less than natural formula I was feeding her. But thrive she did. I let go of my writing to care for Marie. Having done this many times before to care for Nicole I was comfortable with releasing my own plans for a higher purpose. I just relaxed and let go. Nicole and I held Marie day and night. As she became more conscious of the world around her, we played with her between her naps. I whispered and cooed to her about how smart and beautiful she was. I told her I loved her as I kissed and held her.

Lost in my love for this little being, I easily forgot that she was not my own child. I didn't think about how sleeping with Marie, spending every day and night with her, would bond us so deeply to one another. I wasn't trying to bond with her; I was just loving her the way a baby needs to be loved in order to thrive, enveloping her in a cocoon of love. I hadn't anticipated the time when she would leave.

Whenever I walked around town with my tiny charge, people would tell me what a darling baby I had. When I told them that she was my foster child, they would invariably say, "How could you ever give her up! I could never do that." I would smile and say, "I'm just enjoying her so much right now, I'll face that when it comes." I wasn't thinking of the pain of separation. Who thinks about the pain of separation when they're in love?

The phone rang. It was Joyce. She wanted to set up visits for Marie's birth mom, Sarah, and to talk with me about Marie's impending custody trial. I hung up the phone feeling a little edgy.

It wasn't until the first visit with the woman who brought Marie into the world that I became aware of how deep my attachment to her had become. Sarah, Marie's birth mother, and I met at the county children's shelter. Sarah rushed in and grabbed the baby out of my arms, handling Marie roughly and nervously. I felt my maternal instincts come charging forth. Marie, so used to the stillness of my body, cried and looked frightened. I used every ounce of self-control I could muster to not take Marie away from Sarah. I watched but did nothing; my hands were tied. I would never allow someone to handle my own child like this.

It was suddenly dawning on me that I didn't have control of this situation at all. Meeting with Marie's social worker the next day put a match to the dry, hot maternal environment that had developed within me. Joyce was recommending that Marie be made a ward of the court. Teresa, an aunt of Marie's alleged father, Joe, had stepped forward to adopt the baby. The law gives relatives of the birth parents first consideration in adoption. It seems that the healthiest environment for the child is a secondary concern.

I was outraged. Teresa, who was an alcoholic, had a one-year-old baby who was left in child care all day. There were numerous adults moving in and out of the home. How could Teresa provide Marie with the attention and the safety she needed? There were so many people out there who could love and cherish Marie, who was thus far undamaged by neglect or abuse. Aware of how crucial the first few months of life are, I vowed to do everything in my meager power to ensure Marie's safety. I had brought her through the eye of the needle during her first month on this earth. She was here now, felt safe, knew trust.

I felt angry that Marie's fate rested precariously in the hands of strangers. I was angry at the case worker. I was angry at the social service agency and at the judge who, although a stranger to Marie, had the sole power to decide her fate.

I felt caught in what seemed like a hopeless situation. I couldn't let go, yet I refused to accept my powerlessness. I vowed to do whatever I could to see to it that Marie went to a good home, even if I needed to adopt her myself. I interviewed anyone who expressed an interest in her, trying to determine if they would create a good home for her. After a few days I found a couple who were longing to adopt a baby, and the woman would be able to stay at home with her. I called Joyce and carefully broached the subject. I said I had found a couple who wanted the baby. What should they do to be prepared once the child went up for adoption? I wasn't ready for the chastisement I received. This matter was not in my hands, she informed me. The case hadn't even gone to trial yet, and, anyway, if the baby were to go up for adoption there was a list of people from whom the agency would choose.

I was advised not to speak with anyone about the baby, as she was a ward of the court and I needed to observe the rules of confidentiality therein.

I hung up the phone and sat, deflated, with the stark awareness that I really did have no control over Marie's fate. I walked over to Marie's bassinet, where she was beginning to stir. I scooped her up in my arms, brought her to the rocking chair, and rocked and rocked and rocked. I felt her warm, trusting body in my arms, and, aware that any day they could take her from me, I cried. What emptiness! I thought about all the hours I had held her, all the difficult nights when her body struggled to adjust to life outside the womb, and I assured her with my presence that life on earth was worth living. My arms, now full, would soon be empty, and she would be held by someone with a smell different from mine, a different rhythm, a different voice and breathing pattern. It was hard to hold her in my sadness. I wanted to not care about her. I wanted them to take her away, now. I didn't want to bond more deeply; this was painful enough. The Buddha said to a householder who had just lost his child, "So it is householder, so it is! Sorrow, lamentation, pain, grief and despair are born from those who are dear, arise from those who are dear."

I dwelled in sadness for days. I cried easily, couldn't concentrate, and was emotionally distant. Marie sensed my distance and became increasingly difficult to console. Maybe I had lied to her when I assured her that the world was safe. Maybe I had lied to myself when I confidently agreed to simply be an intermediary in this baby's life. Maybe I wasn't cut out for this foster mothering after all. Maybe it was all just too painful.

Slowly I was awakening from my denial about how detached I could be. I was burning through my anger at the thought of anyone hurting this precious baby, having realized that I could not create a perfect world for her. Deep in my sadness, I began to accept that, yes, I love this baby, and, yes, she is only with me for a while. I once again relaxed and could love her with a free and open body and heart.

Only later did I realize that what I had gone through were the classic stages of grief as outlined by the great pioneer in the field of death and dying, Dr. Elisabeth Kübler-Ross. The denial, the anger, the bargaining, the sadness, and, finally, the acceptance, unfolded one by one like petals on a morning glory. While mothering Marie, the stages every parent goes through in letting go of a child as she grows and separates from them were racing through my heart at breakneck speed. I didn't have eighteen years to slowly let go of her; I had to bond and let go of her in a matter of months.

When I was pregnant with Nicole she was my constant companion. Sometimes I wished for some distance from her, to be alone, without the responsibility of this life within me, but I loved being her vessel. When she was expelled from my body into a world of light and pain and brightly colored objects and other people, she knew, for the first time, what it was to be alone, and I too was alone, once again, for the first time in nine months. I had begun the long, sometimes wrenchingly painful, sometimes wonderfully liberating journey of letting go of her a little at a time.

Some losses are to be expected as a healthy part of growth, the baby's birth, the child's first day of school, the child's reaching adolescence, the young adult's leaving home, and getting married, our turning middle-aged, then retiring and reaching old age. Although these losses are natural and healthy they still hurt. My friend Sharon has a son who recently went off to college. She told me how empty the house feels without him, how much she misses their discussions and even things she used to loathe, like his laundry on the floor. She feels an emptiness in her life now that he is gone. She's glad his life is going so well, and she has a full, rich life herself, but still she grieves for what they once had. I remember how I felt on Nicole's first day of school. I drove up to the school. We got out of the car and walked up to the classroom door. There at the door was Nicole's new teacher, who whisked Nicole away from me into a room full of noise and new faces and new activities I would never know. I walked back to the car alone and drove off, empty, glad for the extra time to myself but missing my constant companion.

During the Buddha's time many women entered his spiritual community after the death of their child or children. One such woman, Patacara lost her entire family, a husband, two young children, her parents, and her brothers, in only a few days. She went insane from her sorrow. The Buddha came to her and, with compassion, taught her about the path leading out of suffering. These teachings became her lifeline. The Buddha's compassion and teachings, coupled with her burning willingness to be free from unimaginable suffering, led her to enlightenment. One day as she was pouring water over her feet to wash them, she watched as the water evaporated. In that moment she realized that life is also impermanent. This epiphany freed her mind from attachment and she attained enlightenment.

With each letting go there is sadness and there is freedom. With the baby out of my body I was free to sleep on my stomach, to eat what I wanted to eat, to feel light and singular and empty. When I weaned my baby I was free to sleep at night and to let others feed her, free from the pain of full breasts, free to leave her in someone else's care for more than a few hours. When she went to school I could use that time to read and write and reenter the workforce. With each loss I gained more time to apply to my art and to the world the insights I had gleaned by loving her.

What a blessing it is when the losses come slowly. Gradually our children leave our womb, leave our breast, go to papa, go to school, prefer to be with their friends, and leave home. In order for mothering to be a happy occupation I have needed to learn how to surrender to each separation, to acknowledge and grieve each loss.

There is a Jewish proverb that says "What soap is for the body, tears are for the soul." Grief is a natural part of being human and to deny my grief, whether caused by tragic or expected losses, is to shut the door on a very important aspect of loving. The more I shut the door on grief, push it away from me and try to hold it back, the less fully I am able to embrace her sister, love. Open, expressive grieving cleanses the heart. Some cultures are more comfortable with grieving than others. At Yom Kippur people of the Jewish faith come together as a community and grieve their losses openly and with the full support of their friends and families. In the Anguttara Nikaya the Buddha said, "In all things dear and beloved there will be change and there will be separation from them." In a world where everything that is born dies, where everything that comes to be passes away, cultivating respect for the grieving process allows us to honor that reality and live our lives more fully. When we allow ourselves to go through the full grieving process we keep our hearts open and available for love again and again.

The alternative to feeling the pain of loss is to not love. In *The Prophet,* Gibran writes: "But if in your fear you would seek only love's peace and love's pleasure, then it is better for you that you cover your nakedness and pass out of love's threshing-floor, into the seasonless world where you shall laugh, but not all of your laughter, and weep, but not all of your tears." The less deeply I love, the less loss I feel. In choosing the joy and richness of a life full of love, I need to become comfortable with grief because it is part and parcel of loving.

Sometimes I feel like one of those punching clowns, getting the wind knocked out of me, then bouncing back for more. I will continue to choose love over the fear of pain. Hopefully, through time, I will develop a friendship with grief and humor and wisdom, the wisdom of the fool in love who steps off the precipice without concern for the safety of her resilient heart. However painful it was to lose Marie I didn't want that pain to get in the way of loving anyone else my life is blessed with.

Buddhist nuns and monks are advised against forming attachments. As parents we are invited to become experts at attaching, or bonding, and letting go. Milarepa writes: "All worldly pursuits have but the one unavoidable and inevitable end, which is sorrow: acquisitions end in dispersion; buildings in destruction; meetings in separation; births in death. Knowing this, one should, from the very first, renounce acquisition and heaping up, and building, and meeting; and, faithful to the commands of an eminent guru, set about realizing the Truth."

The nuns and monks may be guides along the spiritual path, yet as householders it would be disastrous for us to apply the principle of nonattachment exactly as they do. It is my job as a mother to attach and let go, feeling the full joy and the full grief of human love.

If mothers were not willing to attach to their babies there would be no future generations. The foster-care movement was set in motion when it became apparent that many children who were put in institutions, who were cared for by a number of different adults instead of one consistent caretaker, died before their first year. The early bonding and attachment between child and adult is essential to a child's survival. As my child bonds, so do I. I give a piece of my time, energy, and love to ensure the survival of my tiny charge. For me, bonding is an act of generosity; for my baby, bonding is survival.

A baby needs to be touched, held, and caressed—the more the better. It is through meeting a baby's needs for touch, nourishment, and warmth that we create a lifelong bond of love. In order to survive, both physically and psycologically, babies need to know that the world is safe; that when they are hungry, food will appear; that when they are wet, they will be made dry; and that when they feel alone, with only the endless air around them, they will be tightly snuggled and held as they were so recently held in the womb. They need to know that the giants who pick them up and move around with them are friendly giants. Then these little ones can relax and grow and begin to feel their own power to navigate in a huge, awesome world.

As parents we hold tightly to our children with the awareness that, sooner or later, they will leave. They are not ours; nothing and no one is. They are temporarily in our care, part of which includes giving up a piece of our heart for them, knowing that they will take that piece of our heart with them when they leave and that we will be left with something missing from our generous and abundant hearts.

On the eve of Marie's departure to her adoptive home I was aware of what a blessing it had been to have Marie spend the first six months of her life with Nicole and me. She opened our hearts and brought more love into our home than I could imagine. I love her dearly and wherever she goes she takes a piece of my heart with her.

FAITH ❧

Patience and Receptivity

I've always been glad I'm a woman. Women should not try to be men. They must refer back to that ultimate greatest strength—the sacrificing, enduring feminine . . . a god-given quality. They need to know the seductive feminine is but a chapter in their lives . . . rather from their highest spiritual femininity they can do anything they want to in the world with grace and harmony. It is a strength that can accomplish anything because it is wisdom, a patience, a waiting, a letting. Hold on to the knowledge, hold on to the idealism, hold on to a deeper faith in the reality of the situation. Holding on and on and on and on in the face of everything in the world; disaster, hatred, crime, prejudice, hold on to this spiritual feminine soul quality because out of it comes wisdom, words to say, gestures to make, deeds to do.

GRANDMA LULA, an anthroposophist,*
at seventy-nine

I thought I knew what cabin fever was during that long Vermont winter. Trapped indoors with my car broken down and no telephone or electricity, I was sure I would go crazy. Night after night, day after day, I amused myself with reading,

---

*Anthroposophy is a movement begun in the late nineteenth century by Rudolf Steiner.

writing, and looking out the window at the bare trees heavy with snow.

Then, one bleak and drizzly winter day, four years later, I was once again inside looking out a window. This time I was aching and nauseous from the flu and had to nurse a feverish cranky baby who couldn't get comfortable. I felt trapped, irritable, and lonely. My husband was out of town, and no relatives were nearby. I wanted someone to take care of me and my baby, but no one was there. So I made a nest for Nicole in my arms and we rocked and rocked for what felt like hours. When she finally gave up the struggle against sleep I carried her limp body to the bassinet and gently laid her down. As soon as she felt my arms move away from her she bolted back into wakefulness, crying tears of utter desolation. Again I took her in my arms and resolved to rock her in that old squeaky chair for the rest of the night.

While I was rocking, wishing I were a child in my mother's arms, looking out the window at the gray sky and pouring rain, day and night melted into one another. I was in a world bounded by four walls, with no time and no companions. I thought of ending it all, and a chill came over me. Each moment felt interminable. Forgotten were the joys of planting a garden or laughing with friends. As much as I loved her, I was feeling trapped by the awesome responsibility of this baby's life in my hands.

There was no way out, no respite, so I stopped resisting the reality of the moment and relaxed into the heart of the experience. As I rocked I felt the back of the chair, my legs curled up in its large, rough, gold-and-green cushion. I heard the squeaking of the chair, felt the rhythm of the rocking. Too exhausted to judge, I saw everything just for what it was. The squeak was a squeak. The rain on the window made large and small drops that I could trace as they slid down the slippery surface of the glass. The squeak wasn't bad or good; it was just a sound. The rain wasn't depressing; it was just large and small drops of water that fell from the sky. I let go of wanting things to be different and surrendered to what was. I felt lightness set in. The rain and my loneliness became beautiful to me.

The first few times I took care of a sick child I felt trapped. Now when I sit all day, even all week, with a sick child, I know that in the future I will laugh with friends and plant a garden. I know now that everything is impermanent and that feeling restless and anxious for things to pass quickly only increases my suffering. Each time I experience impermanence more deeply, a portion of my impatience is chipped away. I remember that I'm sitting here with a sick child and that that is what I'm doing now, not forever. I ground myself with that understanding.

Anicca, dukka, and *annata,* or impermanence, unsatisfactoriness, and egolessness, are the three characteristics of reality according to the Buddha. Insight into the first of these, impermanence, opens the door to the other two. Insight into the impermanence of all things can be found not only during meditation but also during our everyday activities. The Burmese meditation teacher U Ba Khin wrote: "Anicca is, for the householder, the gem of life which he will treasure to create a reservoir of calm and balanced energy for his own well-being and for the welfare of the society." We watch our thoughts arise and fade and see that they are impermanent. We watch our feelings rise and fade and see that they too are impermanent. As we come to see the truth that everything that is born dies, that all that comes into being passes, we can flow with that reality. Peace of mind naturally arises in our consciousness. Life becomes easier even though very little has changed in the external world.

In the beginning of my mothering journey the endurance tests were intense. It was an initiation process in which my ego and body were thrown into the fire repeatedly, often in rapid succession. I had the choice of either defending myself by going into denial, filling up the space with noise and activity, or consciously taking a quantum leap in expanding my boundaries. To accomplish the latter, Buddhism and other spiritual disciplines teach us to enter the unknown with nonjudgmental awareness. Whenever I think back to those times, I think of that lonely winter, rocking my baby in the squeaky rocking chair, because it was then that I learned to be in the moment no matter what it contains. As time went on, meeting the challenges of parenthood became less of a shock. I integrated what I had learned from previous experiences and the wisdom therefrom became a part of me.

When I'm without faith I think that what I am experiencing now is going to last forever. Over time I've developed an awareness of history, of the reality that things are always changing. When a teenager gets a pimple she thinks that her face looks like it's been hit by a meteor shower and that she's doomed to a life of ugliness. With faith she knows that she may have pimples for another week or so but that her skin is going to clear up. Or if I'm in a car and I have to drive five hundred miles with a screaming child in the backseat I know that sometime, somehow, the child will eventually stop screaming. When I'm aware of the fact that the situation I'm in will change, that the present moment has a beginning and ending, then I can keep my sense of humor. I can take a deep breath, count to ten, and watch myself have thoughts of infanticide without getting so attached to those thoughts that I either hate myself or actually hit my child.

It's the difference between going through an experience with my eyes open or keeping them closed. When they are open I see the sights along the way. I see the shape of the experience so that when I am confronted with something similar, I recognize its shape and see the transiency of my immediate situation, like when my baby was teething and becoming feverish, clingy, and cranky.

The first or second time it happened, I worried about the baby, but by the third or fourth tooth, I knew what was happening, what I needed to do about it, and that the discomfort was temporary. I could say "Oh yes, I've been here before. If I only hang in there a little longer I'll soon see the light at the end of the tunnel."

The Pali (an ancient Indian language used in the time of the Buddha) word for "faith" is *Saddha*. It also means "confidence born of conviction." When I've gone through something that is difficult or painful and survive the experience, get back on my feet, and then go through another dark passage, I still feel the pain and despair of what I'm going through but carry the insight gleaned from previous experiences into the darkness of the unknown. Remembering that I have come out of the darkness before bolsters my confidence. I know I will come out of the darkness again. I glimpse the unknown through the known.

Enlightenment can't be explained in any rational terms. It transcends any verbal intellectual construct. But by applying what I've learned from my own experiences, I glimpse enlightenment. This happens most often when I release judgment and watch as love pours into the empty space that I've created. It also happens when I change my perspective and suddenly see things in a clearer, more skillful way. Both these common experiences give me insight into impermanence. In that way the "un-knowable," God or enlightenment, is knowable through Nature—the senses. There are reflections and glimpses of enlightenment all around us, and when we catch these glimpses, they give us the faith to keep moving toward the light.

The reason I have faith that there even is such a thing as enlightenment and that it is worth cultivating is that so many of the spiritual principles I've practiced in motherhood and in everyday life have turned out to be tremendously helpful. This makes me increasingly receptive to wisdom I have not yet experienced firsthand. When I do experience a truth, that knowledge becomes un-shakable for me. In Matthew 17:20 it is written: ". . . for truly I say to you, If there is faith in you even as a grain of mustard seed, you will say to this mountain, Move away from here, and it will move away; and nothing would prevail over you." It takes only a little insight into life to open the door to limitless wisdom, and we all have these little insights daily.

There are times when we all need teachers or mentors, people who have been through what we're now going through and have come out the other end wiser. Such a person can initiate us by say-ing "Just sit." We say, "But I'm going crazy." And the teacher says, " I've never lost a student to insanity yet. Just sit and watch what happens." We argue, "But I don't want to; I hate this. I need some chocolate. I'll be good. I'll do anything just if you let me get up." And the teacher says, "Just sit, you're almost there."

Sometimes we need someone to bolster our confidence and help us see beyond the transciency of our experience. After a few of these experiences we come to know the process. Then we can take a solo flight. That's where faith becomes manifest. I confess that there are many things I'm working toward on the spiritual path that I don't fully understand while I am working on them. I usually don't understand the lesson until I've completed it, so I must make a leap of faith, faith that there is meaning to my expe-riences even if I don't understand it at the moment. Sometimes in order to go through the struggle that accompanies an unfolding insight, the only thing holding me to the path is faith. Not blind faith, which leaves me helpless at my darkest hour, but tangible faith, confidence built on past experiences.

My mother once said to me that she wished she had had the wisdom she has now when she was a young mother. Then she would have been much more patient with her children. I see my-self in the middle of my life cycle, driven to get things done, hardly able to find the time to sit down and play a game with Nicole. Patience comes with wisdom, and wisdom comes with time and experience. That's why it is so valuable to have our elders involved in raising children. I need to be patient with myself in my quest for patience, and elders who have repeatedly approached life's challenges with open minds and hearts can provide me with models along the way.

Faith and patience help me out of self-created prisons of anger, greed, and hatred. Sometimes when I meditate I come across angry thoughts. If I try to push them away, I actually give the anger more power. It's like telling someone "Don't think about a hot fudge sundae with nuts and whipped cream on it." The thought just gets stronger and stronger. When I just sit there with an angry thought, it's just there, and I'm just there with it. I feel it in every cell, and as it becomes familiar to me, I become less resistant to it. As I become more comfortable with the feeling, I know that it will eventually dissipate. This is practicing the patience not to turn away from an unpleasant situation, disciplining myself not to run away from discomfort. When I just sit there with whatever is happening, eventually that particular state of mind fades, and a new one takes its place. When this happens I am grateful for impermanence.

Negativity fades away in the light of insight. Light and insight are always stronger than darkness. Sitting with something as it is, no matter how uncomfortable I get, will eventually dispel it. I sit patiently, or impatiently, with the faith that with the light of awareness my anger will eventually be dispelled. I remind myself that darkness is only the absence of light, nothing more.

Impatience is another expression of anger and hate, all of which have a fiery quality. The Buddha said that anger is like a burning coal that you pick up to throw at someone. The coal may hit your victim or it may not, but in the meantime it is your own hand that gets burned. Isn't it true that when we are most irritated and impatient we are in a great deal of pain?

One fundamental aspect of impatience is product orientation, that is, making the production of a particular outcome or product more important than living in the moment. I want the product and I want it now! If on the way to the store Nicole is stopping to speak with every flower and creature and crack in the sidewalk, I may become angry and impatient with her. I may see her as getting in the way of my objective, which is to make it to the store on time. We live in a results-oriented culture, and whether it's a product or a certain outcome that I want, it is all too easy for me to grow impatient and angry with Nicole's need to explore and enjoy her world. In a less materialistic society being with a child who is learning to walk through this miraculously abundant world is given a higher priority than getting to the store for a product or achieving some short-term result.

Everything in our modern culture encourages us to make, to build, to produce. Not only do we need to do our work perfectly, but we also need to do it with great speed. Not only do we need to put together a superior proposal, but we also need to beat the competition in bringing the product to market. I was taught impatience in school and in the workplace. Then, while parenting or going to church or temple or when meditating, I'm suddenly supposed to possess the virtue of patience.

Just like its sister, perfectionism, impatience has become epidemic, and like perfectionism impatience has its roots in the imbalance of masculine and feminine values. The masculine aspect is aggressive: making, doing, creating. These are all very positive things when balanced with the feminine perspective of receptivity: being, feeling, allowing, relating. Impatience is our masculine aspect's frustration at being called upon to be more passive and receptive, to be present without getting directly involved in the situation.

The feminine aspect balances the masculine with this quality of simply being, with receptivity. In meditation I am in a state of receptivity as opposed to an aggressive creative state. There's nothing to make, nothing to plan, nothing to be done. Just sit! Art, parenting, and spirituality are all fields that demand receptivity; without receptivity in these activities impatience thrives. In such enterprises I spend a lot of time alone, empty, without answers. They all require the ability to relax into not knowing, into receiving the lesson from the situation rather than going into the situation with a preconceived plan to execute as a contractor would carry out the plans for building a house.

I have had to look deeply within myself to see how impatience operates. This inquiry has been well worth the effort. Zengetsu, a Chinese master of the Tang dynasty, wrote: "Virtues are the fruit of self-discipline and do not drop from heaven of themselves as does rain or snow." Practice, practice, practice.

Patience and receptivity are *not* the same as laziness. In our culture, inaction is often associated with weakness and inferiority. The Eastern perspective is quite different. Lao-tzu wrote: ". . . evolved individuals, finally, take no great action, and that is the way the great is achieved." There is potent value in the wisdom that is gained when we are being aware in the moment. A lot of my work as a parent has entailed just *being there.* I've had to learn not to provide solutions to Nicole's problems even while supporting her to find her own solutions. I facilitate Nicole's awareness of her emotions by being a nonjudgmental presence, which not only helps solve the present difficulty but also gives her tools of her own to tap into her feelings and solve future problems without me.

Patience and receptivity are not magical qualities that some lucky people have and the rest of us struggle through life without. They are practical qualities that we can develop. At times it can be like walking a tightrope: remaining active and passive at the same time. While there is no one method for acquiring these skills, the tools we've been discussing throughout this book all bring us closer to this balance.

I am here reminded of the story of Achaan Chah's discourse with a student who confronted him on his apparent inconsistency. Achaan Chah explained that when he sees someone going down a road that he knows well and he is about to fall into a ditch to the right he calls to him to go left. If he sees someone about to fall into a ditch to the left of the road, he calls to him to go right. Guiding students away from extremes and toward the center is the intent of this seemingly contradictory advice. We find balance by being honest with ourselves about which side of the middle we are leaning toward and then taking steps toward the middle.

My cart has the tendency to fall off to the left because I am living in an overly masculinized material era. I have needed to cultivate the feminine art of simply being. If I lived in an overly feminized culture, I would need to develop the masculine aspects of my personality. If not balanced by the feminine, the masculine stresses *doing* to the exclusion of *being*. The feminine, if not balanced by the masculine, can become sentimental, impulsive, and unfocused. I can get overly receptive and process-oriented and end up not accomplishing anything. Mothers know the dilemma of having laundry to do, shopping to do, diapers to change, food to cook, all of which require receptivity and *doing* in great measure. The trick is to be going forward while not going anywhere at all. That's the path of the spiritual aspirant. I'm going somewhere, but where I'm going is right here in the moment.

When I was pregnant I learned a lot about simply being. There is no rushing a baby; birth flows according to Nature's schedules, not mine. Nature is not man-made nor is it man controlled (try as we may!). I waited as morning sickness ran its course. I waited the nine months not knowing when the birth day would come. I waited as the baby settled into sleep at night. Often I had to let go of control, which was not easy. The more I tried to control the situation, the more pain I experienced. There was no relief until I learned to trust that a higher power was guiding the way and that I could, with full confidence, loosen my grip.

Many of us live unhappily and struggle endlessly with phantom demons. These demons need not be the carriers of fruitless suffering. They can be the sandpaper used to smooth out our rough edges. They can be the blessings that irritate us into developing the pearls of compassion and insight. Flowing with the discomfort, using it for enlightenment rather than struggling against it greatly diminishes the growing pains. Patience, patience is the way.

As a parent I learn from my experiences, and Nicole benefits from my example. My friends and I don't always acknowledge the wisdom we've gained by going through the trials that parenting presents. We come out the other end of the parenting experience fundamentally changed. I have seen women change before my eyes as they became pregnant for the first time, gave birth, and became mothers. I watched them become softer, more present. Usually they weren't aware of the changes themselves. The changes seemed to arise, without pretense, like the seasons. It's just Nature's way.

My feminine aspects have been one missing bead on the string of pearls leading to my happiness. Because these beautiful, quiet, receptive qualities do not call attention to themselves, I sometimes overlook them. Our culture claims to value the qualities of patience and receptivity and faith yet regards them as unattainable for mere mortals. I grew up seeing these qualities as lofty ideals, ideals that I believed only saints and mystics were capable of achieving. The truth is that I can know the bliss and well-being of these gentle qualities here and now, wherever I am in my development. I was looking for happiness in something large and lofty while it lay quietly waiting for me in simply being receptive in my everyday life.

MEDITATION ✣

Affirmation and Prayer

The Dhamma of the Buddha is not found in books. If you want to really see for yourself what the Buddha was talking about, you don't need to bother with books. Watch your own mind. Examine to see how feelings come and go, how thoughts come and go. Don't be attached to anything. Just be mindful of whatever there is to see. This is the way to the truths of the Buddha. Be natural. Everything you do in your life here is a chance to practice. It is all Dhamma. When you do your chores, try to be mindful. If you are emptying a spittoon or cleaning a toilet, don't feel as though you are doing it as a favor for anyone else. There is Dhamma in emptying spittoons. Don't feel you are practicing only when sitting still. Some of you complain that there is not enough time to meditate. Is there enough time to breathe? This is your meditation: mindfulness, naturalness in whatever you do.

THE VENERABLE AJAHN CHAH, *Bodhinyana*

I awoke at six in the morning to the sounds of Vivaldi emanating from my alarm clock radio. Pushing down the snooze button, I slept for fifteen minutes more. The violinists, not to be silenced by a reluctant sleeper, started sawing away on their strings once again. And once again I assaulted the snooze button. This dispute over the airwaves went back and forth for three more rounds until I finally admitted defeat at the hands of my relentlessly determined opponent. I stumbled out of bed, brushed my teeth, made tea, drank it, then walked to my meditation chair in a daze. I set the timer for forty-five minutes and sat down.

Settling into my big green chair with my dogs and cats nearby I spoke my prayer out loud:

> There is only one Life. That Life is present everywhere in everybody and everything at all times. That Life is the Abundance of life-forms; that Life is expressed and felt as Love, that Life is the Beauty of this sunrise, the Power of the earth's movement and the Wisdom of each of my cells which contain the intelligence to sustain my body. Since there is only one Life, this Life is who I am. I affirm that I am open to an even deeper insight into the truth that is everywhere present. I accept a release of anything that might get in the way of clarity, calm, and wisdom. Joyfully, gratefully, I release this word knowing it is done now. And so it is.

Then I swept through my body with my mind: "Relaxing my head, neck, shoulders, arms, hands, chest, stomach, bottom, thighs, calves, feet. Straightening my spine, pulling my chin in and neck straight, becoming aware of each part of my body." I felt increasingly alert but still restless and resistant.

Finally, I arrived at the breathing meditation. My mind was acting like it was waiting for a train, twiddling its thumbs. It was going "in, out, in, out . . . I wonder if I should dress warmly today or dress in layers. In, out, in, out . . . Oh no! I forgot to feed the chickens; they're probably out there starving to death, suffering, getting skinnier and skinnier until their eyes fog over and they drop dead. I better feed them right now! OK, OK, OK . . . after I meditate. In, out, in, out . . . I wonder when the bell is going to ring. It should be at least a half hour by now." I was restless. I was impatient. I wanted out. I thought I was going to explode. It's one thing to know about the five hindrances to meditation (doubt, sloth, lust, anger, and the ever-popular restlessness), but it's quite another thing to confront one head on.

During one of my mind's forays, I thought, "Aha! Here's that restlessness I've heard so much about. I don't want to sit here. There are a million things I'd rather be doing, but what a great opportunity to study one of the five hindrances! I'm going to see if I can relax and stay aware of the restlessness until the bell goes off." I settled into watching the feeling of restlessness. The more I watched it, the less it disturbed my concentration. Restlessness became my meditation object. I became tranquil. When the bell sounded, signaling the end of my morning meditation, it surprised me.

Sometimes, when Nicole was young, it was difficult to carve out time in my busy day and to overcome my restlessness long enough to sit down and meditate, but the rewards were always worth the trouble when I did. When I meditate, the thoughts and feelings streaming through my mind come into perspective. Problems that seem huge and insurmountable lose their power, like the little man behind the curtain pretending to be the great Wizard of Oz. I hear more clearly, see more clearly, and am better able to appreciate everything and everyone around me. The amount of activity involved in being a mother and householder makes this time of stillness even more essential for living in a state of clarity.

As I meditate I am strengthening the seven factors of enlightenment: mindfulness, investigation of the truth, effort, rapture, quietude, concentration, and equanimity. As these qualities become stronger in meditation they also become more accessible in my day-to-day activities. My mind becomes crystal clear like a beautiful window allowing me to look out into the world and see my own mind reflected back to me with greater insight.

There are many forms of meditation. Two classical Buddhist practices are Samadi, or concentration meditation, and Vipassana, or insight meditation. While practicing concentration meditation we are focusing our mind on a single object: our own breath, a light, a mantra, chanting—anything that keeps our mind focused on a single point. When we practice Vipassana meditation we are directing our focused minds toward whatever is most insistent at the moment, thereby penetrating deeply into its nature. It is through this penetration into the nature of whatever we are focusing on that insight arises. For instance, while walking, we focus on the feeling of the ground beneath our feet, when a bird sings, shifting our focus to the sound of the bird. While we are focused on the bird, suddenly a strong emotion arises, and we shift our focus to that emotion, and so on. When I gave birth to Nicole the birthing pains were the strongest sensation at that moment, so I focused on them. This kind of focus can bring us into the present no matter what we are doing at the time, sitting in meditation or walking the floor at 3:00 A.M. with a fussy baby in our arms.

When practicing insight meditation we label our experiences and repeat that label three times. For instance, if we smell something we think, "smelling, smelling, smelling." By thinking "smelling" rather than thinking "I am smelling," we detach from the experience and observe it without the notion of self. By repeating the word three times, we give the mind enough time to settle into awareness.

Both forms of meditation, Samadi and Vipassana, are important; they balance one another. The busy mother and householder will find it valuable to practice both forms. Too much concentration without the balance of mindfulness can make the meditator irritable or sleepy. Too much dispersed attention, without the focus of concentration, can lead to distraction and to less focus or presence of mind. In parenting we have constant external demands placed on us. It's easy to get into a state of mind where our thoughts are flitting all over the place as we try to respond to all those demands. Meditation can bring us back to our still center. We can then bring that calm with us into the busyness of our day and stay mindful during the constant activity.

In classical concentration meditation we are developing tunnel vision. Tunnel vision is like a laser beam. It is a narrow, focused mind state needed to break through illusion to reach truth. Another view of Samadi, which may be more useful to mothers who live such stressful, goal-oriented lives, is to think of Samadi as tranquillity instead of concentration, the classical view. Concentration has overtones of *trying* attached to it. Trying creates more tension in the mind, which is not Samadi at all. Instead of thinking of *focusing* the mind or *concentrating,* it might be more helpful to think of *calming* the mind. When our minds are relaxed they don't want to go anywhere and so will focus, be present in the now, naturally. This tranquil mind is content to stay where it is. It is from this soft, relaxed foundation of tranquillity, practiced in an atmosphere of deep awareness and nonjudgmental acceptance of all things, that Vipassana, or insight, arises.

I was once on a retreat that emphasized the classical concentration practice. A woman stood up during the question-and-answer period and asked the teacher how she could increase her concentration. She loved the high it gave her, the bliss, and wanted to hold on to that feeling. The teacher gave her a concentration meditation to practice and sent her on her way to meditate. A few evenings later the same woman got up in front of the group and said that she wanted to meditate all night and asked if someone would stay up with her so she wouldn't be alone. A gentleman who exuded tranquillity and I volunteered. At about midnight I went to get tea and decided to bring some extra cups for the other meditators in case they needed some tea to help them stay awake. I brought the tea in, and the second I sat down the alarm on my watch went off. I was wearing my daughter's watch and had no idea that the alarm had even been set! The timing of the alarm was uncanny. (I have my suspicions that my teacher Anagarika was orchestrating this perfectly timed event from the grave.) The woman, who had been concentrating deeply, jumped at the sound and immediately yelled at me, with fire in her eyes, to stop bothering her. The gentleman sitting with us just looked up at me, smiled, closed his eyes, and kept meditating. It was a wonderful lesson on the problem of too much concentration without enough mindfulness. Although the meditator felt bliss, her bliss immediately turned to anger at the least disruption. Without the proper blend of mindfulness she lacked equanimity. This is why tranquillity may be a more useful way for Westerners to approach Samadi than concentration.

This is one reason it is wise to pick a meditation teacher who is skillful at the practice. Giving a good Dharma talk or sermon is one thing, being skilled at teaching the practice is quite another. A skilled teacher can guide us in turning up the concentration, or turning up the mindfulness at the proper point. It's like tuning a stringed instrument. Finding the midpoint where each string is neither too high nor too low requires skill. As beginners we may find it difficult to guide our own meditation, we are too caught up in the experience and not knowledgeable about the process. It takes someone who is compassionate, someone we trust, someone who is greatly skilled to help us.

If we are going to surrender fully we need a coach whom we trust and the proper situation in which we can relax. A retreat is an excellent opportunity to practice awareness without distractions. When Nicole was young I would leave her with her father once a year and go to Canada on a seven-day retreat with my teacher. That was enough time to recharge my daily practice. On a retreat we let go of everything a busy householder is responsible for: food preparation, shelter, and caretaking. We just meditate.

During retreat my awareness deepens. Through awareness we see that our feelings belong to us and are not created by other people or circumstances outside us. This awareness is the beginning of great personal power. We gain the power to do something about those feelings. As long as we hold onto the illusion that other people or circumstances are responsible for our thoughts and emotions we feel powerless. When we assume responsibility for our thoughts and emotions we can choose to watch them as they dissolve. When Nicole would cry for something she wanted in the store, I sometimes became irritable. When I was able to see that Nicole was not responsible for my feelings of irritability, it was much easier to see those feelings as counterproductive and consciously release them.

I continued other forms of meditation practice when I came home from retreat. Fortunately, sitting is not the only position for meditation. The Buddha taught that enlightenment can be attained in four positions: sitting, walking, standing, and reclining. When we are too busy to sit down on a meditation pillow, this is worth remembering.

Sometimes I would practice Thich Nhat Hanh's beautiful peace meditation when I sat with my foster baby on my lap. She would drink from her bottle as I held her. Meanwhile, I breathed in, feeling the in breath; I breathed out, feeling the out breath. I breathed in, feeling deep; I breathed out, feeling slow. I breathed in, feeling calm; I breathed out, feeling peace. I breathed in, feeling a smile; I breathed out, feeling a release of tension. I breathed in, living in the present moment; I breathed out, into a wonderful moment.

Lying loving-kindness meditation is a form of meditation you can do while lying down. At the end of a challenging day or when you're sick and can't make it out of bed, it can be a godsend. I use it to still my mind before I go to bed. Lying in bed before sleep I wish myself love and happiness. I wish myself good health and a deep tranquil sleep. I think of Nicole asleep in the next room and wish her many friends, a strong healthy body, and the discipline to reach her star. I think of my parents and my brothers and their families and wish them love in their hearts and the peace of knowing they are deeply loved. I think of the neighbors and hope that they all sleep well and deeply, that they will awaken rested and feeling good. I think of all the people in Sonoma and hope they all go to sleep with calm, healthy, happy hearts. I wish all the people in California a roof over their heads and someone who loves them. I wish everyone in the United States safety, love, and shelter. I wish everyone in the world enough to eat, safety, and the feeling of being deeply loved. I wish that all beings in the entire universe complete their own missions with a minimum of suffering and attain the highest enlightenment.

The Venerable Ananda Maitreya, a Buddhist monk, scholar, and meditation teacher, taught us a body-sweeping meditation/ affirmation to help heal the body. I used this healing technique with Nicole when she got old enough to focus her consciousness. Starting with the head, we focus on that area and repeat, "My head is strong and healthy" over and over, visualizing a strong, healthy head. "My neck is strong and healthy, my endocrine system is strong and healthy," and so on, down to our toes. When I was able to truly feel each part of my body as I was focusing on it, I watched that part relax and release any ailment it was carrying. The meditation helped increase my health and energy when I was in the throes of chronic fatigue syndrome. I oftentimes experienced instant healings using this meditation technique.

Being aware is essential to conscious mothering, and meditation practice provides wonderful tools for achieving this awareness regardless of what we are doing. Once I visited my brother, Greg, when he was living in New York City. We were walking down the street, talking, when all of a sudden he stopped in the middle of his sentence exactly at the moment we reached a curb. After a few steps off the curb he continued his sentence. I asked him what made him stop in the middle of his sentence. He told me that every time he gets to a curb he makes it a point to be aware. He was using each curb as his mindfulness object.

Having mindfulness objects in your life can be tremendously helpful. Choose something commonplace, such as the first step into your living room or a decorative object you've placed on a shelf you pass several times a day. Each time you pass the object you can remind yourself to breathe or to remember to be grateful—whatever it is that you need to bring you into the present moment. When driving in your car let each stoplight be your reminder to take an in breath and feel the air moving through your nostrils. Then take an out breath and feel the sensation of the release. Be aware of the sounds around you, and suddenly you are present, aware, and fully alive. Nicole and I keep a mindfulness bell on our mantle above the fireplace. At any time either one of us can strike it, and we both stop and take three breaths. It helps bring both of us back to awareness and is especially helpful during difficult times.

There are many ways to practice meditation while walking. On meditation retreat we practice by walking very, very slowly, watchful of each movement of the body, watchful of the intent to lift the foot, place it on the ground, etc. But you can also do it while walking quickly, staying aware of your body in motion. On retreat you can have the luxury of practicing meditation while walking slowly, which enables you to look closely at the workings of your consciousness. When you walk with a child down the street you can keep bringing your attention back to the feeling of your feet on the ground. It is a blessing to be able to walk on this earth. The blessing is acknowledged by your attention to the present moment.

When I'm alone and have to wait in line I practice a standing meditation. I'm standing in a line at the post office, and the line is so long that people walk in, see it, shake their heads, and walk out. I decide to stay and practice staying aware in each moment. I learned this practice on retreat while waiting in line for meals. Simply deciding to use the potentially anxiety-producing situation of waiting in a line as an opportunity to meditate relaxes my mind immediately. As I practice I notice the tension in my body, and I relax it, body part by body part. I notice my impatience and let go of it. My body becomes relaxed and peaceful. I feel friendlier and smile at the other people in the line. Maybe it's my imagination, but they seem to settle down a bit too.

However it's done, meditation is simply the practice of awareness. We can be aware while sitting on a pillow or a chair or while standing, walking, eating, making love, or while engaged in virtually any activity. If you're a busy householder don't worry about having enough time to meditate. Pay attention. Be aware and you will discover more and more creative opportunities for meditation.

As you become more aware you are also teaching your children the benefits of awareness. You become more present for them and less irritable. Our children see this and may want to meditate as well. Meditation must never be forced on children. They can be invited but never forced, and if they're not ready, we need to just drop it. It's better for our children to find meditation for themselves rather than have bitter associations with spiritual practice later on. Talmudic scholars used to feed their students honey as they studied, emphasizing that learning is sweet. Learning must be sweet to be deeply effective.

For interested children the spiritual teacher Thich Nhat Hanh has developed the following meditation, which works well for youngsters: Breathing in, watching the in breath, breathing out, watching the out breath. Breathing in, "I see myself as a flower"; breathing out, "I feel fresh." Breathing in, "I see myself as a mountain"; breathing out, "I feel solid." Breathing in, "I see myself as water"; breathing out, "I reflect things as they are." Breathing in, "I am like space"; breathing out, "I feel free." Children should be allowed to do this only as long as they wish, even if it's only a minute or two.

There is an important difference among meditation, affirmation, and prayer. In affirmation and prayer we focus on something we desire to change or feel gratitude for. In meditation we don't focus on changing or expressing anything. We are not trying to obtain any information, support, or guidance; we are just there, present with what is. As humans we are developing on many levels. The object of meditation is to end suffering by being in the moment without thoughts or desires. However, when we are in the throes of suffering, either physical or mental, we may need support to release that suffering before we can be fully present in the moment. When that is the case, affirmation and prayer are wonderful tools.

When I was at a low point, feeling that my life was going nowhere, I called my mom on the phone. I poured out my feelings to her, and she gave me this wonderful gift that I would like to share now. She told me that before I go to bed at night and the first thing upon waking in the morning I should say to myself "I am open to receive the people, places, and things I need to fulfill my highest good." It's a wonderful affirmation because it doesn't assume that I know what is best for me or that what I currently think of as fulfillment is the deepest fulfillment to be had. Affirmations can be very powerful, especially if there is a lot of heart and conviction behind the words.

After a week of practicing my mom's affirmation nothing special had happened, but I persisted. After the second week I met a woman who was to become a dear and lasting friend. I would never have thought to ask for a friend, yet upon meeting her I felt fulfilled. Of course, fulfillment is not dependent on changes in outer circumstances. That can be one of the pitfalls of affirmations: They can slip into willfulness and desire for more things and possibly for things that are not useful to us on our path. Maybe getting sick is a blessing if we need to slow down and look at something or develop more compassion. Blessings come in many disguises. When we make affirmations we need to release attachment to outcome and stay open to an outcome that may be wiser than anything we may be able to imagine at the moment. It sometimes takes practice, sometimes trial and error, to recognize exactly what that means and how to do it.

I had a friend who visualized herself surrounded by money. She ended up getting hired as a bank teller! That wasn't exactly what she had in mind, but it was exactly what she affirmed. It's important to be clear and specific with imagery. We receive what we believe, both negative and positive. Each thought is a prayer. The more we learn to direct our thoughts, the more we can have a positive effect on our destinies. Through meditation we learn the meaning of attachment, letting go, and trust, and those teachings prepare us not only for living with awareness but also for using affirmations and prayer constructively.

We often get caught up in relative truths, the things we wish to change in our everyday lives, and forget absolute truth, the divinity that is always at our core. A prayer is an affirmation of absolute truth as it applies to a given situation. The literal meaning of the word *prayer* in Aramaic, the language of the original scriptures, is "to set a trap." The Aramaic scholar Rocco A. Errico writes: "In the East, when men went hunting, they would get a box, some bait, and a string. They'd then hide behind a rock or some other adequate shelter, still holding the string, and wait patiently for the animal they desired to trap. And when the animal came, they'd pull the string and catch the prey. So prayer, then, literally means 'to set your mind like a trap and wait patiently to catch the thoughts of God; that is, to trap inner guidance and impulses.'"

Every night, when Marie, my foster daughter, was with me, I would pray that she would find a good permanent home. The matter was out of my hands. All I could do was appeal to the highest outcome. The prayer for Marie was fueled by the fire of my heart's desire. She ended up in the loving home of a couple who were unable to conceive. Prayer is an effective tool for reprogramming our thinking and ultimately coming into alignment with our true Divine nature. It can help prepare the ground where insight can thrive.

The Hindu saint Holy Mother was honored in India because "Though a householder, she never deviated from the ideal of renunciation laid down for monks. She did not shun disagreeable duties nor did she welcome agreeable ones. Through all her activities, she never forgot God." Similarly, Mother Teresa said, "You should spend at least half an hour in the morning and an hour at night in prayer. You can pray while you work. Work doesn't stop prayer, and prayer doesn't stop work." Through prayer we release negative repetitive thoughts and replace them with positive life-affirming ones. We pluck the weeds and plant the seeds of a beautiful garden that will feed us abundantly.

Meditation, affirmation, and prayer are practices, not religions. A Christian can meditate and still remain a Christian, and a Buddhist can pray and still practice Buddhism. Consider this thought: "If the heart wanders or is distracted, bring it back to the point quite gently and replace it tenderly in it's master's presence. And even if you did nothing during the whole of your hour but bring your heart back and place it again in Our Lord's presence, though it went away every time you brought it back, your hour would be very well employed." It was spoken by Saint Francis of Sales and uses the words "Our Lord's presence," thus identifying it as being of Christian origin. Otherwise it could just as easily have been the words of a Buddhist meditation instructor uttered during an interview with a student.

Meditation, affirmation, and prayer are tools designed to help develop loving kindness, clarity of mind, equanimity, and awareness. We are wise to use all the tools at our disposal regardless of their source. If something can help us love more deeply, see more clearly, and gain wisdom, what does it matter if it comes from Judaism, Christianity, Islam, Hinduism, or Buddhism? We are fortunate to have access to these practices and even more fortunate if we use them toward the attainment of outer well-being and inner peace.

UNIVERSAL MOTHERING

Peace

The scent of flowers is carried
No farther than the wind allows,
Neither the sandalwood, tagar, nor jasmine.
But the fragrance of the deeds of good men spreads,
To the ends of the earth, in all directions,
Regardless of the wind.

DHAMMAPADA

Unlimited, unconditional love, a mind as clear and simple as light streaming through a window on a winter morning, a comfortable faith that life is unfolding perfectly, the ability to take whatever life hands us and make a feast out of it—these are not just for the precious few born at the perfect time and into the perfect conditions for enlightenment. If you and I are enlightened enough to want these qualities, we are enlightened enough to have them.

In Carl Sandburg's book *Rootabaga Stories,* Bubbles sends a telegram to Hatrack the horse stating "Anybody can walk hundreds of miles putting one foot ahead of another." Staying on the path, bit by bit, our work in the world falls into place. We don't need to force our growth and expansion. It is far more effective to meld into enlightenment, to become receptive and let our work enter us. The feminine principle makes itself known not with aggressiveness but with receptivity.

When I was on retreat at a Catholic convent in Canada some years ago, there was a poster I kept passing in the hall with the message "Bloom where you are planted." The phrase stuck with me. It dawned on me that I didn't need to go to far-off exotic places or engage in strange unfamiliar practices to become enlightened. I don't have to wait until I'm financially solvent. I don't have to wait until I can find the right teacher or until my child grows up or until I retire and finally have time to sit down and meditate. I don't need to wait for anything to happen to become enlightened. I can become enlightened right here where I am, right now, as I engage in mothering and householding.

While mothering I am increasing my capacity to love, widening my capacity to give, developing the wisdom that can only emerge from a rich life lived with an open heart. I am becoming more flexible. Like a willow tree, I am blown and shaped by the winds of the changes I am required to make in order to parent more effectively while staying rooted in my values. I am becoming strong from doing all those things I didn't believe I was capable of doing but did anyway out of love for my family.

When I became a parent I received the precious gift of insight into unconditional love. I had the choice of keeping that radiance confined within my own four walls or using it as a starting point for developing a boundless love for all beings. I've learned how to love from being Nicole's mother. I can now radiate that love out to my audience when I sing, to the person in line in front of me at the post office, and to all others, both known and unknown.

Using the map of my spiritual practice I have come to trust the basic goodness of life. This map puts the life lessons gained on my mothering journey into perspective, shedding light on the meaning of my experiences. The light cast on the pains and joys of everyday life has deepened my ability to love. It doesn't matter whether one draws inspiration from the Bible, from a Buddhist monk or nun, or from the Koran or the Torah. True spiritual wisdom nourishes and supports spiritual growth. For me, Buddhism has accelerated the process of enlightenment as I use the insights into unconditional love that I learned from mothering to deepen my awareness.

Mother Teresa, in reference to a question asked about the wisdom of setting up rescue centers in wealthy Western nations said, "People today are hungry for love, for understanding love which is much greater and which is the only answer to loneliness and great poverty. That is why we are able to go to countries like England and America and Australia where there is no hunger for bread. But there people suffer from great loneliness, great despair, terrible hatred, feeling unwanted, feeling helpless, feeling hopeless. They have forgotten how to smile, they have forgotten the beauty of the human touch." It is feminine spiritual energy, mother love, which can heal them.

A spiritually conscious mother sees behind the masks of differences into the heart of sameness. She can provide the nourishment this troubled world so sorely needs. Her heart has been stretched open to the pain and joy of loving to the point where all beings become her children. By her shining example, she brings peace to her community, the hospitals, the courtrooms, the stage, the classrooms, the Senate, and the marketplace. The world is hungry for her milk.

And as she continues extending her love to herself, to her home and family, to her community, and to the world, she comes to a place where her mothering path drops away and all that is left is the sound of the wind through the pines and a full moon in a cloudless sky.